CHILDREN'S *Living* SPANISH
ILLUSTRATED LESSON BOOK

by MARY FINOCCHIARO
Illustrations by CLAUDINE NANKIVEL

Crown Publishers, Inc., New York

THE LIVING LANGUAGE COURSES®

Living Spanish
Living French
Living Italian
Living German
Living Japanese
Living Russian
Living Portuguese (South American)
Living Portuguese (Continental)
Living Hebrew
Children's Living French
Children's Living Spanish
Advanced Living French
Advanced Living Spanish
Living English for Native Spanish Speakers
Living English for Native French Speakers
Living English for Native Italian Speakers
Living English for Native German Speakers
Living English for Native Portuguese Speakers

Additional Living Language™ conversation manuals and dictionaries may be purchased separately.

Copyright © 1986, 1960 by Crown Publishers, Inc.

All rights reserved. No part of this book may be reproduced or transmitted in any form or by any means, electronic or mechanical, including photocopying, recording, or by any information storage and retrieval system, without permission in writing from the publisher.

Published by Living Language, a division of Crown Publishers, Inc., 225 Park Avenue South, New York, New York 10003.

LIVING LANGUAGE is a trademark and THE LIVING LANGUAGE COURSE is a Registered Trademark of Crown Publishers, Inc.

Manufactured in the United States of America

Library of Congress Catalog Card Number: 60-8616

ISBN 0-517-56335-5

1986 Updated Edition

10 9 8 7 6 5 4

INTRODUCTION

The fresh, open minds of children are ideally suited for foreign language study. Child development experts agree that children have the capacity to learn a new language much more easily than adults.

The best way for children to learn a new language is the same way they mastered their native tongue—that is, through hearing, speaking, and using the language at home and at play, in a variety of situations. The lessons contained in the *Children's Living Spanish* course are centered around everyday experiences that children can easily understand.

Each lesson begins with an introductory paragraph that poses a question in English; the answer to the question is revealed as the lesson progresses in Spanish. Young students are encouraged to use their talent for mimicry by repeating after the native instructors.

Key phrases and important vocabulary words are repeated throughout the text. It is these essential expressions that the child will be able to master. The lessons build upon one another, becoming increasingly complex. Naturally, the young student is not expected to retain all the language in the recordings. In some cases, words are included chiefly to create smooth dialogue and are there for recognition, rather than active repetition.

Three well-known children's stories are included in the course. Read at a normal speed, the stories help with listening comprehension and build the student's vocabulary. At the end of each lesson, songs and games reinforce the learning process in a lively way.

With *Children's Living Spanish*, young students will have fun learning about another culture as well as learning a new language. This early introduction will help pave the way for the study of Spanish and other languages in the future.

We sincerely hope you find this course to be useful and enjoyable.

Children's Living Spanish contains the following:

- Two one-hour cassettes containing a total of 40 lessons
- An *Illustrated Lesson Book* in which all of the recorded material is given in Spanish and English
- A *Picture Dictionary* containing illustrations and definitions of the most important vocabulary from the recordings

LESSON CONTENT

The lessons are composed almost entirely of dialogues centered around the everyday life of a child. They cover all four seasons, so young students learn to speak about the circus in spring, picnics in summer, Halloween in fall, and Christmas in winter.

The main action of each lesson is illustrated. The pictures, coupled with the introductory paragraph in English, orient the students to the theme of each lesson. The Spanish dialogue that follows is heard on the recording. Many of the lessons conclude with a song or poem, which children should join in singing or reciting.

Simple tests are periodically included in the course. These help motivate students and serve as an indicator of their progress. Parents and teachers, however, are encouraged to devise their own quizzes (questions, drawings, matching of pictures) to reinforce the learning process. If children clearly understand all the information in the lessons and can write in English, the parent or teacher may want to introduce them to written Spanish.

Since the material is intended for children, the familiar *tu* form is used when children are speaking with one another. In addition, several lessons include the polite and plural forms of address (*usted* and *ustedes*).

Most of the speakers on the recordings use a Latin American pronunciation, although Castilian Spanish is used occasionally so that students can hear the different accents.

The lessons present aspects of both Latin American and North American culture. Latin American traditions, like breaking the piñata and the presentation of Christmas gifts by the Three Kings on January 6, are introduced alongside the preparation of a jack-o-lantern and the arrival of Santa Claus. Children will be able to learn about other cultural traditions as well as their own and talk about them in a new language.

Listed below are some ways you can help children learn Spanish:

1. Learn Spanish with them (if you don't already know it). Naturally, we suggest *Living Spanish: The Complete Living Language Course®* for adult beginners.

2. Show enthusiasm and approval for children's ability to imitate the speech in the recordings.

3. Read the introductory paragraph to the children (if they cannot yet read) or let them read the paragraph aloud to you.

4. Help young students recall personal experiences related to the theme of the lesson they are working on.

5. Ask them to tell you something in Spanish about the words in the *Picture Dictionary*.

6. Encourage them to add other pictures to the *Picture Dictionary* or to start a scrapbook.

7. Try not to expect too much too soon. Learning another language takes time, repetition, and practice.

INSTRUCTIONS

Place Cassette 1, Side 1 in your tape recorder. There are 10 lessons on each side of each cassette and they are separated by a prolonged pause so you can stop the machine and have the next lesson lined up and ready to use.

Turn to **Lección 1** on page 9 in this *Illustrated Lesson Book*. You will see only the Spanish text, preceded by a short paragraph in English and accompanied by one or more drawings. The introductory paragraph and drawings are designed to set the scene for the conversation you will hear. Try to follow in the printed text the sounds you hear on the recording. Whenever there is a pause at the end of a phrase or sentence, repeat what you have heard.

Try to figure out the meaning of what you have heard, and see if you know the English equivalent to the individual words. Then turn to the English translation of the Spanish conversation. See how much of the meaning and how many of the words you interpreted correctly. Remember, Do not look at the English until after you have tried to determine the meaning of the Spanish.

Now turn back to the Spanish, rewind the cassette to the beginning of the lesson, and repeat the phrases after the speakers once more. See if you know the meaning of each phrase. If not, look at the English again and repeat the procedure until you are satisfied with your progress. Follow the same method with the next lesson.

When you come to songs, just listen the first time you hear them. Then try to sing the song along with the voice on the cassette. You will find this to be one of the most pleasing ways to learn Spanish. The stories that are told in Lessons 6, 7, 25, 26, 31, and 32 are recorded without the pauses that allow you to repeat. It will help you, however, to try to read the story along with the speaker after you have heard it once. Reading aloud will improve both your pronunciation and listening comprehension.

Don't forget that the more frequently you listen and repeat, the more material you will remember and the longer you will retain it.

If you are unsure of the meaning of any word in the lesson, look it up in the

Picture Dictionary. You will find its English meaning as well as a picture to make it clear. To help you say things in Spanish, there is also an English/Spanish section in the *Picture Dictionary.*

To help you remember words, there are many Word Study lists. Here you will find only the Spanish word and picture. If you do not know the meaning of any words in these lists, look it up in the *Picture Dictionary.*

There are several quizzes in the course. Try to answer all the questions as well as you can. The results will help you see your progress.

Buena suerte! Good Luck!

CONTENTS

	Introduction	3
LESSON 1	BUENOS DÍAS, DORMILONA	9
LESSON 2	DIEZ DEDITOS	11
LESSON 3	¿QUÉ HORA ES?	13
LESSON 4	PREPÁRATE PARA EL DESAYUNO	15
LESSON 5	Mmmm—PANQUÉS	17
LESSON 6	LÉEME UN CUENTO, POR FAVOR	19
LESSON 7	LOS TRES OSOS	23
LESSON 8	¿PUEDO SALIR AHORA?	27
LESSON 9	¿A QUÉ VAMOS A JUGAR?	29
LESSON 10	¿QUIERES VER MI PERRO?	31
LESSON 11	¿UN GATO TAMBIÉN?	33
LESSON 12	NO PUEDO JUGAR HOY	35
LESSON 13	CUIDADO CON LAS LUCES	37
LESSON 14	A LA COMPRA	39
LESSON 15	EN LA PASTELERÍA	41
LESSON 16	SÓLO UN JUEGO, MAMÁ	43
LESSON 17	¡LO TENGO!	45
LESSON 18	ENCANTADA, SEÑORA	47
LESSON 19	ME GUSTA TODO	49
LESSON 20	¿AYUDAS A TU MAMÁ?	53
LESSON 21	¡QUÉ COMIDA TAN RICA!	55
LESSON 22	¿EN QUÉ CANAL?	57
LESSON 23	VAMOS A JUGAR A LA ESCUELA	59
LESSON 24	¿CÓMO SE DICE?	61
LESSON 25	LOS TRES CERDITOS	63
LESSON 26	¿QUIÉN TIENE MIEDO AL MAL LOBO GRANDE?	65
LESSON 27	¿QUIERES VENIR A UNA FIESTA?	69
LESSON 28	LA FIESTA DE CUMPLEAÑOS	71
LESSON 29	¿QUIÉN PUEDE ROMPER LA PIÑATA?	73
LESSON 30	¡AY, AY, TENGO DOLOR DE ESTÓMAGO!	75
LESSON 31	CAPERUCITA ROJA	77
LESSON 32	¿QUIÉN TIENE MIEDO? ¿YO? ¡OH, NO!	79
LESSON 33	VIENE EL CIRCO	81
LESSON 34	UN PICNIC	83
LESSON 35	A LA PLAYA	85
LESSON 36	UNA CARTA DE LOS ABUELOS	87
LESSON 37	LA FINCA DE LOS ABUELOS	89
LESSON 38	¡QUIQUIRIQUÍ!	91
LESSON 39	QUIERO UN ÁRBOL GRANDE, GRANDE	93
LESSON 40	FELIZ NAVIDAD Y FELIZ AÑO NUEVO	95

ABOUT THE AUTHOR

Professor Mary Finocchiaro is one of the most qualified language educators in our school system. Author of numerous books and magazine articles dealing with language instruction; Associate Professor of Education; Director of the Foreign Language Institute of Hunter College; Fulbright Professor in the Methods of Teaching Language; Chairman of Foreign Languages, Secondary Schools; Supervisor of the Language Program for Junior High Schools; Consultant to the New York State Department of Education; Consultant to the Government of Puerto Rico—these are only some of the posts Professor Finocchiaro holds or has held.

LECCIÓN 1

BUENOS DÍAS, DORMILONA

Would you like to meet a Spanish-speaking family? We know they'll become your friends very soon. One of the children of the family is a real sleepy head. Oh, how she hates to get up in the morning! Do you?

Mamá—Buenos días, Elena.
Elena—Buenos días, mamacita.
Mamá—Levántate, Elena. Es tarde.
Elena—¿Es tarde? ¿Qué hora es?
Mamá—Son las nueve.
Elena—¿Son las nueve ya?
Mamá—Sí. Son las nueve.
Papá—Buenos días, Elena. ¿Cómo estás?
Elena—Buenos días, papacito. Buenos días, Carlitos. ¿Cómo estás, hermanito?
Papá—Dame un beso, Elena. Hasta luego.
Elena—Hasta luego, papacito. Hasta luego, Carlitos.
Mamá—Levántate, Elena.
Elena—Sí, mamacita, pronto.

Vamos a cantar:

Buenos días, mamacita
Buenos días, papacito
Buenos días, hermanito
Buenos días, Elena.

LESSON 1

GOOD MORNING, SLEEPY HEAD

Mother—Good morning, Helen.
Helen—Good morning, Mother dear.
Mother—Get up, Helen. It's late.
Helen—It's late? What time is it?
Mother—It's nine o'clock.
Helen—It's nine o'clock already?
Mother—Yes. It's nine o'clock.
Father—Good morning, Helen. How are you?
Helen—Good morning, Father dear. Good morning, Charlie. How are you, brother dear?

Father—Give me a kiss, Helen. See you later.
Helen—See you later, Father. See you later, Charlie.
Mother—Get up, Helen.
Helen—Yes, Mother dear, right away.

Let's Sing!
Good morning, Mother dear,
Good morning, Father dear,
Good morning, brother dear,
Good morning, Helen.

WORD STUDY

hermanito (el)

mamacita

levántate

papacito

LECCIÓN 2

DIEZ DEDITOS

Would you like to know how Mexican children learn numbers? Listen carefully for the little poem that tells us how.

Mamá—Elena, es tarde. ¿Estás lista?
Elena—No, mamacita. ¿Qué hora es?
Mamá—Son las nueve y media. Levántate.
Elena—¿Son las nueve y media ya? Es tarde. Tengo una idea mamacita. Enséñame a decir la hora.

Mamá—Es una buena idea. Primero vamos a aprender los números. Escucha: uno, dos, tres, cuatro, cinco, seis, siete, ocho, nueve, diez. Repite los números, Elena.

Elena—Uno, dos, tres—
Mamá—Continúa: cuatro, cinco . . .
Elena—Cuatro, cinco, seis . . . Mamacita. ¿Cuál número ahora?
Mamá—Siete. Espera, Elena. Hay un verso español con los números. Escucha:

> Uno, dos, tres, cho
> Cuatro, cinco, seis, co
> Siete, ocho, nueve, late
> Bate, bate el chocolate.

Elena—¡Qué bueno, mamá! Tienes razón. Ahora, es fácil recorder los números. Escucha, mamacita:

> Uno, dos, tres, cho
> Cuatro, cinco, seis, co
> Siete, ocho, nueve, late
> Bate, bate el chocolate.

Mamá—Muy bien, Elena. Vamos a continuar con los números más tarde.

LESSON 2

TEN LITTLE FINGERS

Mother—Helen, it's late. Are you ready?
Helen—No, Mother dear. What time is it?
Mother—It's nine-thirty. Get up.
Helen—It's nine-thirty already? It is late. I have an idea, Mother dear. Teach me to tell time.
Mother—It's a good idea, but first let's learn the numbers. Listen—One, two, three, four, five, six, seven, eight, nine, ten. Repeat the numbers, Helen.
Helen—One, two, three. . . .
Mother—Continue—four, five—
Helen—Four, five, six . . . Mother dear, what number now?
Mother—Seven. Wait, Helen. There is a Spanish verse with the numbers. Listen:
    One, two, three, cho
    Four, five, six, co
    Seven, eight, nine, late
    Beat, beat the chocolate.
Helen—Goody, goody (How nice), Mother. Now it's easy to remember the numbers. Listen, Mother dear:

    One, two, three, cho
    Four, five, six, co
    Seven, eight, nine, late
    Beat, beat the chocolate.

Mother—Very good, Helen. Let's continue with the numbers later.

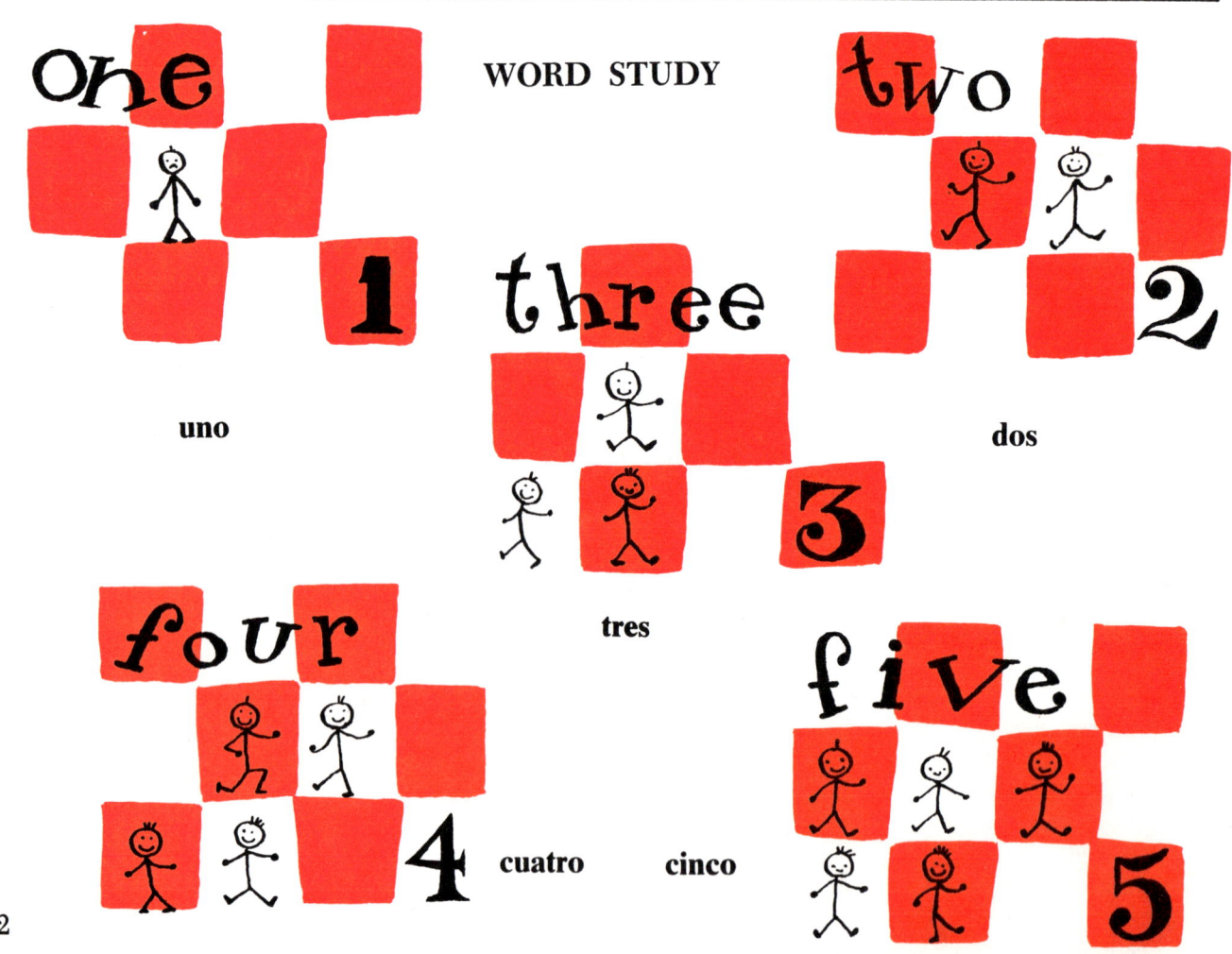

WORD STUDY

one 1 uno

two 2 dos

three 3 tres

four 4 cuatro

five 5 cinco

LECCIÓN 3

¿QUÉ HORA ES?

Telling time is important in any language. How else would we let our friends know when we can meet them in the playground, or in the park?

Elena—Mamacita, ya sé los números del uno al diez. Escucha—uno, dos, tres, cuatro, cinco, seis, siete, ocho, nueve, diez.
Mamá—Muy bien, Elena.
Elena—Enséñame a decir la hora.
Mamá—Bien, Elena. Mira este reloj. Es la una. ¿Qué hora es, Elena?
Elena—Es la una.
Mamá—Mira este reloj. Son las tres. ¿Qué hora es, Elena?
Elena—Son las tres, mamacita. ¿Qué hora es en este reloj, mamacita?
Mamá—Son las seis y media. Repite, Elena: son las seis y media.
Elena—Son las seis y media . . . ¿Qué hora es en este reloj, mamacita . . . ? Yo sé, yo sé: Son las   . . .

Mamá—Espera, Elena. Es el mediodía o es la medianoche. De día, es el mediodía. De noche, es la medianoche.
Elena—Mamá, quiero jugar. ¿Quieres jugar conmigo?
Mamá—Sí, Elena.
Elena—Bueno. Estoy pensando en una hora. ¿Cuál es?
Mamá—¿Es la una?
Elena—No. No es la una.
Mamá—¿Son las seis y media?
Elena—Sí, mamá. Son las seis y media.

Vamos a cantar:
Dos y dos son cuatro
Cuatro y dos son seis
Seis y dos son ocho
Y ocho, diez y seis.

LESSON 3

WHAT TIME IS IT?

Helen—Mother dear. I know the numbers from one to ten. Listen—one, two, three, four, five, six, seven, eight, nine, ten.
Mother—Very good, Helen.
Helen—Teach me to tell time.
Mother—Now Helen, look at this watch. It's one o'clock. What time is it, Helen?
Helen—It's one o'clock.
Mother—Look at this watch. It's three o'clock. What time is it, Helen?
Helen—It's three o'clock, Mother dear. What time is it on this watch, Mother dear?
Mother—It's six-thirty. Repeat, Helen, It's six-thirty.
Helen—It's six-thirty . . . What time is it on this watch, Mother dear? . . . I know, I know it's . . .

Mother—Wait, Helen. It's noon or mid-night. By day, it's noon. By night it's mid-night.
Helen—Mother, I want to play. Do you want to play with me?
Mother—Yes, Helen.
Helen—Good. I'm thinking of a time. Which is it?
Mother—Is it one o'clock?
Helen—No, it's not one.
Mother—Is it six-thirty?
Helen—Yes, Mother. It's six-thirty.

Let's Sing!

Two and two are four
Four and two are six
Six and two are eight
And eight sixteen.

QUIZ 1

Let's make sure we've understood what we've learned so far. We're going to ask you to do something. Try to answer these questions in Spanish, then compare your answers with those on page 16.
1. Repite los números del uno al cinco.
2. Repite los números del cinco al diez.
3. Mira cada (each) reloj.

¿Qué hora es?

¿Qué hora es?

¿Qué hora es?

¿Qué hora es?

LECCIÓN 4

PREPÁRATE PARA EL DESAYUNO

It's so nice to look spic and span in the morning. Let's find out how Helen does it.

Elena—Mamá, tengo hambre. Quiero mi desayuno, por favor.
Mamá—Primero, prepárate. Lávate la cara y las manos.
Elena—¿Dónde está mi jabón, mamá?
Mamá—Aquí está.
Elena—¿Dónde está mi toalla?

Mamá—Aquí está. Lávate los dientes ahora.
Elena—¿Dónde está mi cepillo de dientes?
Mamá—Aquí está tu cepillo de dientes. Pero, ¿qué te pasa, Elena? ¿Dónde está?, ¿dónde está?
Elena—Perdóname, mamá. Estoy pensando en el juego con el reloj. Mira, mamá. Mírame ahora la cara, las manos y los dientes.

Mamá—Muy bien, Elena. Dame tu cepillo para el cabello.
Elena—Aquí está, mamacita.
Mamá—Ahora, dame una cinta, por favor. Ahora, dame tu falda y tu blusa.
Elena—Aquí está mi falda y aquí está mi blusa.
Mamá—Mira en el espejo, Elena. Ahora, tú eres mi niña querida.

LESSON 4

GET READY FOR BREAKFAST

Helen—Mother, I'm hungry. I want my breakfast, please.
Mother—Get ready first. Wash your face and hands.
Helen—Where's my soap, Mother?
Mother—Here it is.
Helen—Where's my towel?
Mother—Here it is. Wash your teeth now.
Helen—Where's my tooth brush?
Mother—Here's your tooth brush. But what's the matter with you, Helen? Where is? Where is?
Helen—I'm sorry, Mother. I'm thinking of the game with the watch. Look, Mother. Look at my face, my hands and my teeth now.
Mother—Very good, Helen. Give me your hairbrush.
Helen—Here it is, Mother dear.
Mother—Now, give me a ribbon, please. Now, give me your skirt and your blouse.
Helen—Here is my skirt and here is my blouse.
Mother—Look into the mirror, Helen. Now, you are my darling daughter.

ANSWERS TO QUIZ 1

1. Uno, dos, tres, cuatro, cinco
2. Cinco, seis, siete, ocho, nueve, diez
3. Es la una y media.
   Son las tres.
   Son las diez.
   Es el mediodía.

LECCIÓN 5

Mmmm — PANQUÉS

Are your eyes bigger than your stomach? Helen's are! You'll never guess what she doesn't want. Mmmm.

Mamá—Vamos a comer ahora, Elena.
Elena—Sí, mamacita, por favor. Ahora tengo mucha hambre. Son las diez y media ya.
Mamá—Yo lo sé. Levántate más temprano.
Elena—¿Qué hay para mi desayuno?
Mamá—Una sorpresa.
Elena—¿Una sorpresa? ¿Qué es? ¡Mmmm! Panqués. ¡Qué bueno! Muchas gracias, mamacita.

Mamá—Siéntate a la mesa y ponte tu delantal.
Elena—¿Dónde está mi delantal?
Mamá—Aquí está.
Mamá—¿Qué quieres con los panqués, jarabe o mermelada?
Elena—Jarabe y mantequilla, mamá.
Mamá—Aquí están los panqués.
Elena—¿Sólo tres panqués, mamá? Yo tengo mucha, mucha hambre.
Mamá—Hay tres más en este plato.
Elena—Los panqués son muy ricos, mamá, con jarabe y mantequilla.
Mamá—¿Qué quieres tomar—leche o chocolate?
Elena—Mm. Vamos a ver. Chocolate, por favor.
Mamá—Aquí está el chocolate y aquí hay tres panqués más.
Elena—Mamá, cómetelos tú. Son muy ricos.
Mamá—¡Ja, ja! Elena, comes más con los ojos que con la boca.

Vamos a cantar:

Mamá is mother
Ocho eight
Papá is father
Tarde late.

17

LESSON 5

M-M — PANCAKES!

Mother—Let's eat now, Helen.
Helen—Yes, mother dear, please. Now I'm very hungry. It's ten-thirty already.
Mother—I know it. Get up earlier in the morning.
Helen—What is there for my breakfast?
Mother—A surprise.
Helen—A surprise? What is it? Mm, pancakes. How nice! Many thanks, Mother dear.
Mother—Sit at the table and put on your apron.
Helen—Where is my apron?
Mother—Here it is.

Mother—What do you want with the pancakes, syrup or marmalade?
Helen—Syrup and butter, Mother.
Mother—Here are the pancakes.
Helen—Only three pancakes, Mama? I'm very, very hungry.
Mother—There are three more on this plate.
Helen—The pancakes are very delicious, mother, with syrup and butter.
Mother—What do you want to drink, milk or chocolate?
Helen—Mm. Let's see. Chocolate, please.
Mother—Here's the chocolate and here are three more pancakes.
Helen—Mother, you eat them. They're delicious.
Mother—Ha, ha. Helen, your eyes are bigger than your stomach.

Let's Sing!

Mamá is mother
Ocho—eight
Papá is father
Tarde—late

QUIZ 2

Do we understand everything so far? Let's make sure.

Say *Sí* if the sentence is correct and *repeat the correct sentence.*

Say *No* if the sentence is *not* correct. If you say *No*, give what you think is the right answer. Then turn to page 21 and compare answers.

1. Elena dice: Mamá, tengo hambre.
2. Hay panqués para el desayuno.
3. Elena quiere tomar leche.

LECCIÓN 6

LÉEME UN CUENTO, POR FAVOR

Do you know that boys and girls everywhere in the world enjoy the same fairy tales? Do you have a favorite story that you like to hear over and over again? Helen does. Would you like to find out what it is?

Elena—Mamacita, no quiero salir ahora. Léeme un cuento, por favor.
Mamá—¿Cuál quieres oír?
Elena—Vamos a ver. Sí, yo sé cuál. El cuento de Los Tres Osos.
Mamá—Bueno. Siéntate aquí.

Los Tres Osos

Había una vez tres osos: un oso grande, el papá; un oso mediano, la mamá; y un oso pequeño, el niño. Los tres osos viven en una casa en un bosque.

En la casa de los tres osos hay tres camas: una cama grande para el oso grande; una cama mediana para el oso mediano, y una cama pequeña para el oso pequeño.

En la casa hay también tres sillas: una silla grande, una silla mediana, y una silla pequeña para el oso pequeño.

En la casa hay también una mesa. En la mesa hay tres platos: un plato grande, un plato mediano, y un plato pequeño para el oso pequeño.

En la mesa hay tres cucharas: una cuchara grande, una cuchara mediana, y una cuchara pequeña para el oso pequeño.

Un día el oso grande dice:
"—Tengo hambre."
El oso mediano dice:
"—Yo tengo mucha hambre."
Y el oso pequeño repite:
"—Yo tengo mucha hambre también."
La mamá prepara la comida. Prepara una sopa rica y sabrosa. El oso grande toma la cuchara grande, prueba la sopa y dice:
"—¡La sopa está caliente!"
El oso mediano toma la cuchara mediana, prueba la sopa y dice:
"—¡Sí, la sopa está muy caliente!"
El oso pequeño toma la cuchara pequeña, prueba la sopa y dice:
"—¡Sí, sí, la sopa está muy caliente!"
El oso grande dice:
"Vamos a dar un paseo por el bosque. Vamos a tomar la sopa más tarde."
El oso mediano dice:
"—Sí, vamos a dar un paseo por el bosque."
El oso pequeño repite:
"—Sí, sí, vamos a dar un paseo por el bosque."

(continued)

LECCIÓN 6

Los tres osos van al bosque. Dejan la puerta de la casa abierta. Una niña entra en la casa de los tres osos.

"—Mmm . . . ¡Qué sopa tan rica! Tengo hambre,"—dice la niña.

Toma la cuchara grande, prueba la sopa que hay en el plato grande y dice:

"—¡Esta sopa está muy caliente!"

Entonces toma la cuchara mediana, prueba la sopa que hay en el plato mediano y dice:

"—¡Esta sopa está muy caliente también!"

Entonces toma la cuchara pequeña y prueba la sopa que hay en el plato pequeño y dice:

"—¡Esta sopa es muy buena!," —y se toma toda la sopa que hay en el plato del oso pequeño . . .

Elena—Continúa, mamá.
Mamá—Carlitos llora. Vamos a ver por qué llora. Vamos a continuar el cuento más tarde.

LESSON 6

READ ME A STORY, PLEASE

Helen—Mother dear. I don't want to go out now. Read me a story, please.
Mother—Which do you want to hear?
Helen—Let's see. Yes, I know which one. The story of The Three Bears.
Mother—Good. Sit here.

The Three Bears

Once upon a time there were three bears: a big bear, the father; a medium-sized bear, the mother; and a small bear, the child. The three bears live in a house in a forest.

In the house of the three bears there are three beds: a big bed for the big bear, a medium-sized bed for the medium-sized bear and a small bed for the small bear.

In the house, there are also three chairs: a big chair, a medium-sized chair and a small chair for the small bear.

In the house, there is also a table. On the table, there are three plates, a big plate, a medium-sized plate and a small plate for the small bear.

On the table, there are three spoons: a big spoon, a medium spoon and a small spoon for the small bear.

One day, the big bear says, "I'm hungry."

The medium-sized bear says, "I'm very hungry."

And the little bear repeats, "I'm very hungry, too."

The mother prepares the meal. She prepares a delicious and tasty soup.

The big bear takes the big spoon, tries the soup and says, "The soup is hot."

The medium-sized bear takes the medium-sized spoon, tries the soup and says, "Yes, the soup is very hot."

The small bear takes the small spoon, tries the soup and says, "Yes, yes. The soup is very hot!"

The big bear says, "Let's take a walk through the forest. Let's have the soup later."

The medium-sized bear says, "Yes, let's take a walk through the forest."

The small bear repeats, "Yes, yes. Let's take a walk through the forest."

(continued)

ANSWERS TO QUIZ 2

1. *Sí*. Elena dice: Mamá, tengo hambre.
2. *Sí*. Hay panqués para el desayuno.
3. *No*. Elena quiere tomar chocolate.

LESSON 6

The three bears go to the forest. They leave the door of the house open.

A girl enters the house of the three bears. "Mm. What delicious soup! I'm hungry," says the girl.

She takes the big spoon, tastes the soup in the big plate and says, "This soup is very hot."

Then she takes the medium-sized spoon, tastes the soup in the medium-sized plate and says, "This soup is very hot, too!"

Then she takes the small spoon and tries the soup in the little plate and says, "This soup is very good," and she drinks up all the soup in the small bear's plate.

Helen—Continue, Mother.
Mother—Charles is crying. Let's go see why he is crying. Let's continue the story later.

WORD STUDY

panqués (los)

jarabe (la)

oso (el)

casa (la)

grande

LECCIÓN 7

LOS TRES OSOS

Have you listened to the first part of the story carefully? Would you know how to tell someone what happens next in English? Let's find out how Spanish-speaking children would tell what happens next.

Elena—Mamá, por favor continúa el cuento de Los Tres Osos ahora.
Mamá—Bueno, Elena. Siéntate en esta silla. Vamos a ver. ¿Dónde estamos?
Elena—Mamá, la niña está ya en la casa.
Mamá—Muy bien. Escucha.

. . . La niña ve las tres sillas. Está muy cansada. Se sienta en la silla grande y dice:

"—Esta silla no es cómoda."
Se sienta en la silla mediana y dice:
"—Esta silla no es cómoda."
Entonces se sienta en la silla pequeña y dice:
"—Esta silla es muy cómoda."
Pero la silla es muy pequeña y se rompe.
La niña dice entonces:
"—Tengo sueño."
Se acuesta en la cama grande y dice:
"—Esta cama no es cómoda."
Se acuesta en la cama mediana y dice:

"—Esta cama no es cómoda."
Se acuesta en la cama pequeña y dice:
"—Esta cama es muy cómoda"—, y la niña se duerme.

Un momento después los osos entran en la casa.

El oso grande ve su cuchara y su plato y dice:
"—¡Alguien entró aquí y probó mi sopa!"
El oso mediano ve su cuchara y su plato y dice:
"—¡Sí, alguien entró aquí y probó mi sopa también!"
El oso pequeño ve su cuchara y su plato y dice:
"—¡Sí, sí, alguien entró aquí y se tomó toda mi sopa!"
Entonces el oso grande ve su silla y dice:
"—¡Alguien entró aquí y se sentó en mi silla!"

(continued)

LECCIÓN 7

Y el oso pequeño dice:

"—¡Sí, sí, alguien entró aquí y rompió mi silla!"

El oso pequeño llora.

Entonces el oso grande ve su cama y dice:

"—¡Alguien entró aquí y se acostó en mi cama!"

El oso pequeño ve su cama y dice:

"—¡Sí, sí! ¡Mamá! ¡Papá! ¡Hay una niña en mi cama!"

Los tres osos van a la cama del oso pequeño.

En este momento la niña abre los ojos, ve a los tres osos y grita:

"—¡Ay! ¡Tengo miedo!"

La niña se levanta de la cama, sale y corre, corre por el bosque.

LESSON 7

THE THREE BEARS

Helen—Mother, please continue the story of The Three Bears now.
Mother—Good, Helen. Sit down in this chair. Let's see. Where are we?
Helen—Mother, the girl is already in the house.
Mother—Very well, listen.

The girl sees the three chairs. She is very tired. She sits in the big chair and says, "This chair is not comfortable."

She sits in the medium-sized chair and says, "This chair is not comfortable."

Then she sits in the small chair and says, "This chair is very comfortable."

But the small chair is very small and it breaks.

The girl then says, "I'm sleepy."

She lies down on the big bed and says, "This bed is not comfortable."

She lies down on the medium-sized bed and says, "This bed is not comfortable."

She lies down on the small bed and says, "This bed is very comfortable," and the girl falls asleep.

A moment later the three bears enter the house.

The big bear sees his spoon and his plate and says, "Someone has entered here and has tasted my soup."

The medium-sized bear sees her spoon and plate and says, "Yes. Someone has entered here and has tasted my soup, too."

The little bear looks at his spoon and plate and says, "Yes. Yes. Someone has entered here and has drunk all my soup."

Then the big bear sees his chair and says, "Someone has entered here and has sat down in my chair."

(continued)

WORD STUDY

comida (la)

sopa (la)

mediano

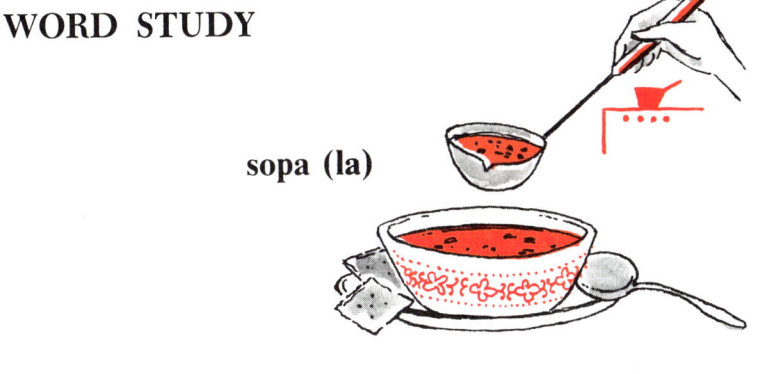

bosque (el)

LESSON 7

And the little bear says, "Yes, yes. Someone has entered here and has broken my chair." The little bear cries.

Then the big bear sees his bed and says, "Someone has entered here and has lain down on my bed."

The little bear sees his bed and says, "Yes, yes, Mama, Papa. A girl is in my bed!"

The three bears go to the bed of the little bear.

At that moment, the girl opens her eyes, sees the three bears and cries, "Oh! I'm afraid."

The girl gets up from the bed and runs, runs through the forest.

WORD STUDY

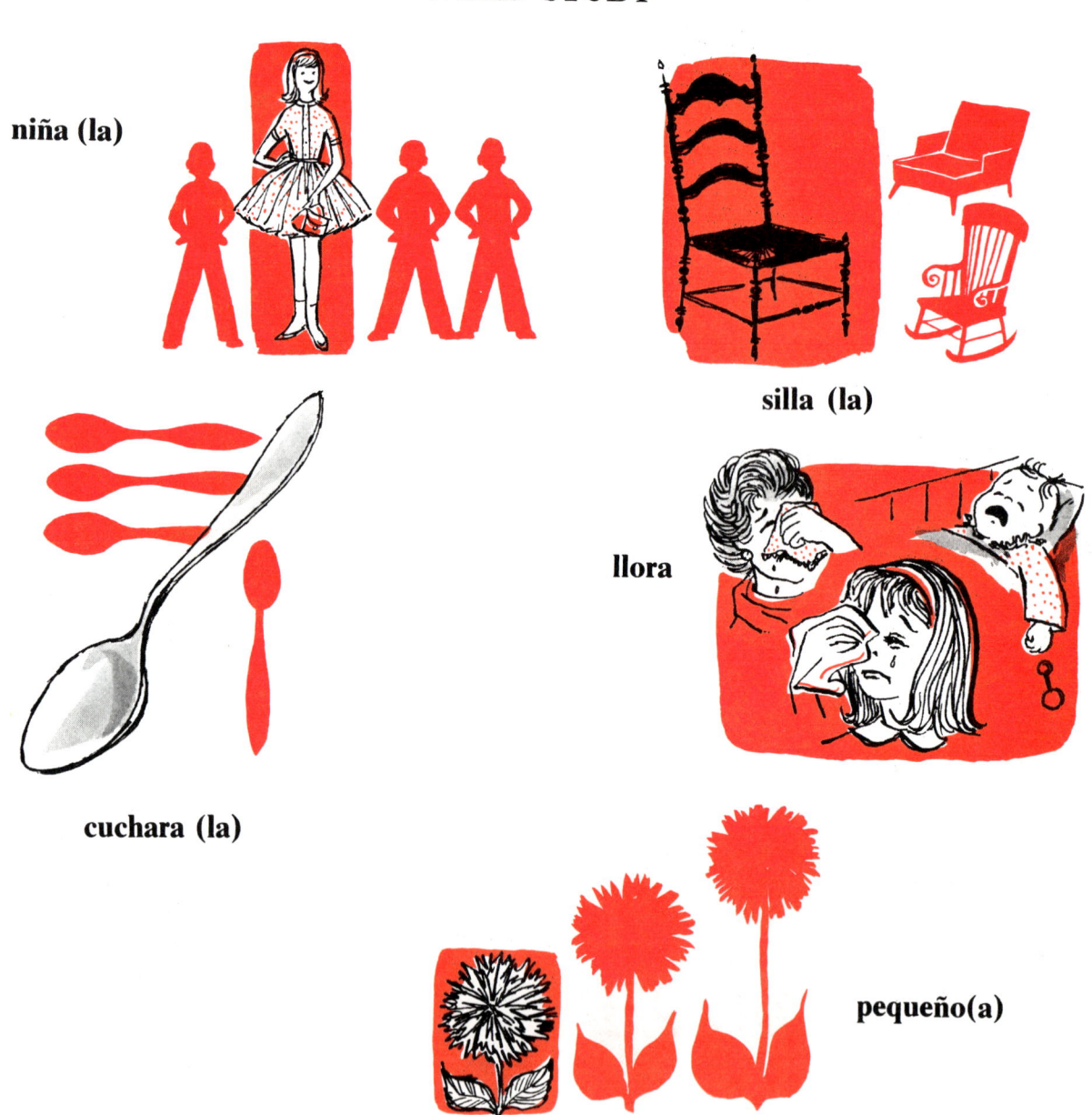

niña (la)

silla (la)

cuchara (la)

llora

pequeño(a)

LECCIÓN 8

¿PUEDO SALIR AHORA?

Spanish-speaking children have many verses and poems which make asking questions fun. Listen for the poem which you can use to ask a new boy or girl on your street what his or her name is.

Elena—Mamacita, ¿puedo salir ahora, por favor? Quiero jugar con mis amigas.

Mamá—Sí, Elena, puedes salir. ¿Cómo se llaman tus amigas?

Elena—Una se llama Juana; una se llama Rosa; y una se llama Susana.

Mamá—¿Hay sólo niñas? ¿No hay niños?

Elena—Sí, hay uno.

Mamá—¿Cómo se llama?

Elena—Se llama Roberto.

Elena—Mamá. ¿Qué me pongo?

Mamá—Ponte el sobretodo, el sombrero de lana, los pantalones de lana y los guantes.

Elena—¿Mi sobretodo, mis pantalones de lana y mis guantes? ¿Por qué, mamá? Hace calor.

Mamá—Hace calor en la casa. Afuera no hace calor.

Elena—Bueno, mamá. ¿Dónde está mi sobretodo?

Mamá—Aquí está.

Elena—¿Dónde están mis pantalones?

Mamá—Aquí están.

Elena—¿Dónde están mis guantes?

Mamá—Pero Elena, ¿qué pasa? Siempre ¿dónde están? ¿dónde están? ¿No sabes dónde está tu ropa? Está en tu armario.

Elena—Perdóname, mamá. Tienes razón.

Mamá—Dame un beso. Regresa a la una. Vamos a almorzar a la una hoy.

Elena—Sí, mamacita. Hasta luego.

¿Quieres recitar conmigo?

    A E I O U
    Arbolito del Perú
    Yo me llamo Elena
    ¿Cómo te llamas tú?

LESSON 8

MAY I GO OUT NOW?

Helen—Mother dear, may I go out now, please? I want to play with my friends.
Mother—Yes, Helen, you may go out. What are your friends' names?
Helen—One is named Joan; another is named Rose, and another is named Susan.
Mother—Are there only girls? Aren't there any boys?
Helen—Yes, there is one.
Mother—What's his name?
Helen—His name is Robert. Mother, what shall I put on?
Mother—Put on your coat, your woolen hat, your woolen pants and your gloves.
Helen—My coat, my woolen pants, and my gloves? Why, Mother? It's warm.
Mother—It's warm in the house. It's not warm outside.
Helen—All right, Mother. Where's my coat?
Mother—Here it is.
Helen—Where are my pants?
Mother—Here they are.
Helen—Where are my gloves?
Mother—But Helen, what's the matter? Always where are, where are? Don't you know where your clothing is? It's in your closet.
Helen—I'm sorry, Mother. You're right.
Mother—Give me a kiss. Come back at one o'clock. We're going to have lunch at one o'clock today.
Helen—Yes, Mother dear. See you later.

Would you like to recite with me?

AEIOU
Little tree of Peru
My name is Helen
What's your name?

WORD STUDY

amigo (el)

sobretodo (el)

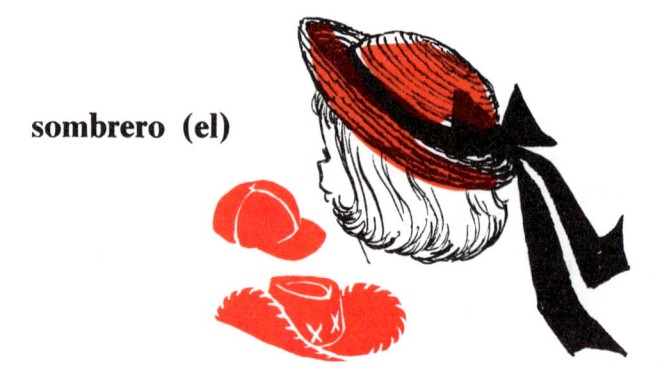

sombrero (el)

pantalones (los)

LECCIÓN 9

¿A QUÉ VAMOS A JUGAR?

Robert would like to join in the fun again. Do you think he'll be able to? I wonder.

Elena—Buenos días, Rosa.
Rosa—Buenos días, Elena.
Elena—Buenos días, Juana.
Juana—Buenos días, Elena.
Rosa—¡Ah, mira! Aquí está Susana.
Todas—Buenos días, Susana.
Susana—Buenos días, Elena. Buenos días, Rosa.
Elena—¿A qué vamos a jugar?
Susana—Vamos a saltar la comba.
Rosa—Bueno. Susana va a saltar primero.
Todas—Vamos a contar. Uno, dos, tres, cuatro, cinco. ¡Oh, oh, Susana! ¡Un error!

Susana—Ahora le toca a Elena.
Todas—Uno, dos, tres, cuatro, cinco, seis, siete, ocho, nueve, diez. Muy bien, Elena.

Roberto—Buenos días, niñas.

Todas—¡Vete, Roberto! No vamos a jugar contigo nunca más.
Roberto—Miren. Tengo una sorpresa.
Todas—¿Una sorpresa? ¿Qué es?
Roberto—Miren. Es un pajarillo.

Todas—¡Un pajarillo! ¡Qué lindo!—Roberto, queremos jugar contigo. Quieres dar a la comba o quieres saltar?
Roberto—Quiero saltar primero.

Vamos a cantar:

Pajarillo Barranqueño

Pajarillo pajarillo
Pajarillo barranqueño
¡Qué bonitos ojos tienes!
Lástima que tengan dueño.

LESSON 9

WHAT ARE WE GOING TO PLAY?

Helen—Good morning, Rose.
Rose—Good morning, Helen.
Helen—Good morning, Joan.
Joan—Good morning, Helen.
Rose—Oh, look. Here's Susan.
All the girls—Good morning, Susan.
Susan—Good morning.
Helen—What shall we play?
Susan—Let's jump rope.
Rose—Good. Susan will jump first.
All the girls—Let's count. One, two, three, four, five. Oh, oh, Susan, a mistake.
Susan—Now, it's Helen's turn.
All the girls—One, two, three, four, five, six, seven, eight, nine, ten. Very good, Helen.
Robert—Good morning, girls.
All the girls—Go away, Robert. We're not going to play with you ever again.
Robert—Look. I have a surprise.
All the girls—A surprise? What is it?
Robert—Look. It's a little bird.
All the girls—A little bird. How pretty! Robert, we want to play with you. Do you want to hold the rope or do you want to jump?
Robert—I want to jump first.

Let's Sing!

Little bird of the cliffs
Little bird of the cliffs
What beautiful eyes you have
What a pity they have a master.

QUIZ 3

Now we will play a little game. Make a drawing after each of the four Spanish words, showing what they mean to you. Then turn to the page in the dictionary shown beside the word in the manual and see if you can find the drawing and Spanish word.

1. Dibuja un *auto*.
   (See dictionary page 5)

2. Dibuja los *pantalones*.
   (See dictionary page 34)

3. Dibuja los *guantes*.
   (See dictionary page 23)

4. Dibuja un *pajarillo*.
   (See dictionary page 34)

LECCIÓN 10

¿QUIERES VER MI PERRO?

Robert would like Helen to visit him at home to see his other pets. What do you think Helen has to do before she can accept Robert's invitation?—You're right. She has to get her mother's permission.

Elena—Roberto, ¡qué pajarillo tan bonito!
Roberto—Tengo un perro muy bonito también.
Elena—¿Un perro? ¿Puedo ver tu perro?

Mamá—Bueno, Roberto vive cerca.
Elena—¿Puedo ir, mamacita?
Mamá—Sí, Elena. Puedes ir. Regresa a la una en punto.

Roberto—Sí, con mucho gusto. Ven conmigo.
Elena—Primero voy a pedir permiso a mi mamá.
    Mamá, mamá. Este es Roberto Pérez. Roberto tiene un perro muy bonito. Yo quiero ver el perro de Roberto. Por favor, mamá.
Mamá—Elena, espera, espera. Mucho gusto, Roberto.
Roberto—Mucho gusto, señora.
Mamá—Bueno, y ¿dónde está el perro?
Roberto—Está en mi casa, señora.
Mamá—¿Dónde vives, Roberto?
Roberto—Vivo en la calle de León, número ocho.

Elena—Sí, mamá. ¿Qué hora es ahora?
Mamá—Es el mediodía.
Elena—Voy a regresar a la una en punto.
Roberto—Gracias, señora. Adiós.
Mamá—Adiós, Roberto. Recuerdos a tu mamá.
Roberto—Gracias, señora.

Vamos a cantar:

Calle is street
Cuchara spoon
Adiós good bye
Mediodía is noon.

31

LESSON 10

DO YOU WANT TO SEE MY DOG?

Helen—Robert, what a pretty little bird.
Robert—I have a very pretty dog, too.
Helen—A dog? May I see your dog?
Robert—Yes, certainly (with much pleasure). Come with me.
Helen—First, I must ask my mother's permission.
Helen—Mother, Mother. This is Robert Perez. Robert has a very pretty dog. I want to see Robert's dog. Please, Mother.
Mother—Helen, wait, wait. Happy to meet you, Robert.
Robert—Happy to meet you, ma'am.
Mother—Good, where's the dog?
Robert—It's in my house, ma'am.
Mother—Where do you live, Robert?
Robert—I live on Leon Street, number eight.
Mother—Good. Robert lives nearby.
Helen—May I go, Mother dear?
Mother—Yes, Helen. You may go. Come back at one o'clock sharp.
Helen—Yes, Mother. What time is it now?
Mother—It's noon.
Helen—Thanks, Mother. I'll return at one o'clock promptly.
Robert—Thank you, ma'am. Good-by.
Mother—Good-by, Robert. Regards to your mother.
Robert—Thank you, ma'am.

Let's Sing!

Calle is street
Cuchara—spoon
Adios—good-by
Mediodia is noon.

WORD STUDY

jugar

salta

pajarillo (el)

perro (el)

LECCIÓN 11

¿UN GATO TAMBIÉN?

Did you ever hear the expression, "They fight like cats and dogs"? Robert hasn't only heard it, he lives with it nearly every day. Let's find out why.

Roberto—Mamá, ésta es mi amiga, Elena Sánchez.
La Mamá de Roberto—Mucho gusto, Elena.
Elena—Mucho gusto, señora.
Roberto—Mamá, Elena quiere ver el perro.
Elena—Sí, por favor, señora.
La Mamá de Roberto—Pasa, pasa, Elena. Dame tu sobretodo y tus guantes, Elena. Dame tu sobretodo y tus guantes también, Roberto. Y tu sombrero, por favor.

Elena—¡Qué perro tan bonito, Roberto! ¿Cómo se llama?
Roberto—Se llama Chico.
Elena—Buenos días, Chico. ¿Cómo estás? Mira, Roberto, Chico me da la pata. Roberto, ¿tienes un gato también?

Roberto—Sí.
Elena—¿Dónde está? Quiero ver el gato también.

Roberto—Aquí está debajo de la mesa. Está tomando su leche.

Elena—¡Qué gato tan bonito! ¿Cómo se llama?
Roberto—Se llama Nolo.
Elena—Buenos días, Nolo. Roberto, ¿dónde está Chico?
Roberto—Está corriendo por la casa. Tiene celos del gato.
Elena—¡Qué lástima! ¿Qué hora es, Roberto?
Roberto—Es la una.
Elena—¿Es la una ya? ¡Qué lástima! Tengo qué correr. Adiós, Roberto. Adiós, Chico. Adiós, Nolo.

Vamos a cantar:

¿Adónde, adónde ha ido mi perro?
Adónde, adónde se fué?
Con las orejas bajas
Y cola también
¿Adónde, adónde se fué?

LESSON 11

A CAT, TOO?

Robert—Mother, this is my friend, Helen Sanchez.
Robert's Mother—Happy to meet you, Helen.
Helen—Happy to meet you, ma'am.
Robert—Mother, Helen wants to see the dog.
Helen—Yes, please, ma'am.
Robert's mother—Come in, come in, Helen. Give me your coat and your gloves, Helen. Give me your coat and your gloves too, Robert, and your hat, please.
Helen—What a pretty dog, Robert. What's his name?
Robert—His name is Chico.
Helen—Hello (Good morning) Chico. How are you? Look, Robert, Chico is giving me his paw. Robert, do you have a cat, too?
Robert—Yes.
Helen—Where is it? I want to see the cat too.
Robert—Here he is—under the table. He's drinking his milk.
Helen—What a pretty cat. What's his name?
Robert—His name is Nolo.
Helen—Hello (Good morning), Nolo. Robert, where is Chico?
Robert—He's running around the house. He's jealous of the cat.
Helen—What a shame! What time is it, Robert?
Robert—It's one o'clock.
Helen—It's one o'clock already? What a pity! I must run. Good-by, Robert. Good-by, Chico. Good-by, Nolo.

Let's Sing!

Where, where has my dog gone?
Where, where did he go?
With his ears drooping
And his tail too
Where, where did he go?

WORD STUDY

mesa (la)

gato (el)

guantes (los)

LECCIÓN 12

NO PUEDO JUGAR HOY

Are there any special kinds of cookies that you like more than others? Our friends do. Let's let them tell us about their favorite kind in a song they'll sing for us.

Mamá—Elena, ve a la puerta.
Juana
Susana   } Buenos días, Elena.
Roberto

Elena—Buenos días, Juana. Buenos días, Susana. Buenos días, Roberto.
Juana
Susana   } ¿Puedes salir, Elena? ¿Puedes jugar con nosotros?
Roberto
Elena—No, no puedo. Viene una amiga de mamá. Tengo que ayudar a mi mamá.
Mamá—¿Quién es, Elena?
Elena—Mamá, son Juana, Susana, y Roberto. Quieren jugar conmigo.
Mamá—Elena no puede jugar hoy. Elena tiene que ayudar en la casa. Pero tengo una idea. Elena puede salir.
Juana
Susana   } ¡Qué bueno, señora!
Roberto
Elena—¡Puedo salir, puedo salir! Gracias, mamacita.
Mamá—Necesito muchas cosas de las tiendas. Pueden ir todos a la compra, si quieren.
Juana
Susana   } Sí, señora, con mucho gusto.
Roberto
Elena—Sí, mamá, con mucho gusto. ¿Qué necesitas, mamá?
Mamá—Vamos a ver. Necesito pan, azúcar, un bizcocho, y jalea.

Elena—Mmm, un bizcocho. ¿Qué clase de bizcocho, mamá?
Mamá—Un bizcocho de chocolate, por favor. Necesito galletas también. Voy a preparar la lista.
Todos—Mmm, galletas. Me gustan mucho las galletas.

Vamos a cantar:

Me gustan todas
Me gustan todas
Me gustan todas en general
Pero galletas, pero galletas
Si son de coco me gustan más.

35

LESSON 12

I CAN'T PLAY TODAY

Mother—Helen, go to the door.

Joan, Susan, Robert—Good morning, Helen.

Helen—Good morning, Joan, good morning, Susan, good morning, Robert.

Joan, Susan, Robert—Can you come out? Can you play with us today?

Helen—No, I can't. A friend of Mother's is coming. I must help my mother.

Mother—Who is it, Helen?

Helen—Mother, it's Joan, Susan, and Robert. They want to play with me.

Mother—Helen can't play today. Helen must help at home. But I have an idea. Helen can go out.

Joan, Susan, Robert—What luck, ma'am.

Helen—I can go out, I can go out. Thanks, Mother dear.

Mother—I need many things from the stores. You can all go shopping if you wish.

Joan, Susan, Robert—Yes, ma'am gladly.

Helen—Yes, Mother, gladly. What do you need, Mother?

Mother—Let's see. I need bread, sugar, a cake and jam.

Helen—Mm, a cake. What kind of cake, Mother?

Mother—A chocolate cake, please. I need cookies, too. I'm going to prepare a list.

All the children—Mm, cookies. I like cookies very much.

Let's Sing!

I like them all.
I like them all.
I like them all, in general.
But the cookies, I like best,
Are the coconut ones.

QUIZ 4

Can you answer these questions? Try them. Then compare your answers with those on page 38.

1. ¿Dónde vive Roberto?
2. ¿Dónde está el perro?
3. ¿Dónde está el gato?
4. ¿Cómo se llama el gato?

LECCIÓN 13

CUIDADO CON LAS LUCES

Mother appreciates it when you can go on errands for her. But what does she worry about? Traffic, of course. Mothers everywhere in the world are the same, as you will see.

Mamá—Elena, aquí está la lista.
Elena—Vamos a ver. Dos botellas de leche, cinco libras de azúcar, pan blanco, dos tarros de jalea . . . ¿De qué sabor, mamá?
Mamá—Un tarro de jalea de uvas y un tarro de jalea de fresas. Continúa leyendo la lista.
Elena—Un bizcocho de chocolate, una libra de galletas. ¿Dónde compro el azúcar?
Mamá—En la tienda de comestibles.
Elena—¿Y dónde compro la leche y el pan?
Mamá—En la tienda de comestibles.

Elena—¿Dónde compro la jalea? ¿En la tienda de comestibles también?
Mamá—Sí, Elena.
Elena—¿Dónde compro el bizcocho y las galletas?
Mamá—En la pastelería. Aquí tienes diez dolares.

Elena—¿Es todo, mamá? ¿No necesitas más?
Mamá—No, no necesito más. Cuidado con las luces. Pasen sólo si la luz está verde. No pasen si la luz está roja.

Elena—No te apures, mamá.
Mamá—Niños, regresen todos aquí. Voy a preparar galletas y chocolate para todos.
Todos—¡Qué bueno! Gracias, señora. Regresamos pronto. Hasta luego.

¿Quieres aprender más?

Más is more
Pan is bread
Puerta is door
Rojo is red.

37

LESSON 13

WATCH THE LIGHTS

Mother—Helen, here's the list.
Helen—Let's see. Two bottles of milk, five pounds of sugar, white bread, two jars of jam. What flavor, Mama?
Mother—One jar of grape jam and one jar of strawberry jam. Continue reading the list.
Helen—A chocolate cake, a pound of cookies. Where shall I buy the sugar?
Mother—In the grocery store.
Helen—And where shall I buy the milk and the bread?
Mother—In the grocery store.
Helen—Where shall I buy the jam? In the grocery store also?
Mother— Yes, Helen.
Helen—Where shall I buy the cake and the cookies?
Mother—In the Pastry Shop. Here are ten dollars.
Helen—Is that all, Mother? You don't need anything else?
Mother—No, I don't need anything else. Watch the lights! Walk only if the light is green. Don't walk if the light is red.
Helen—Don't worry, Mother.
Mother—Children, all of you come back here. I'm going to prepare cookies and chocolate for all the children.
All the children—Fine! Thanks, ma'am. We'll return right away. See you later.

Do you want to learn more?

Más is more
Pan is bread
Puerta is door
Rojo is red.

ANSWERS TO QUIZ 4

1. Vive en la calle de León, número ocho.
2. Está en la cocina.
3. Está debajo de la mesa.
4. Se llama Nolo.

LECCIÓN 14

A LA COMPRA

Do you like to go shopping? Try to prepare your list in Spanish next time you go. It will be easy for you and such fun.

Elena—Buenos días, señor.
Tendero—¿Qué deseas?
Elena—Deseo dos botellas de leche, cinco libras de azúcar, y pan blanco.
Tendero—Aquí tienes la leche, el azúcar, y el pan blanco. ¿Deseas algo más?

Tendero—¿Es todo?
Elena—Sí. Creo que sí. Aquí tiene diez dólares.
Tendero—Muchas gracias. Aquí tienes la vuelta. Adiós. Buenos días.

Elena—Voy a leer mi lista. ¡Ah, sí! Deseo dos tarros de jalea.
Tendero—¿De qué sabor?
Elena—Un tarro de uvas y uno de fresas.
Tendero—¿Deseas un tarro grande o pequeño?
Elena—¿Hay un tarro mediano?
Tendero—Sí, hay un tarro mediano.
Elena—Entonces, el tarro mediano, por favor.

Elena—De nada, señor. Adiós.
Tendero—¿Y tú, niña? ¿Qué deseas?
Susana—Nada, señor. Vengo con Elena.
Tendero—Y tú, niño, ¿qué deseas?
Roberto—Nada, señor. Vengo con Elena.
Tendero—Buenas tardes, niños. Cuidado con las luces. Pasen sólo si la luz está verde.
Todos—Sí, señor. Adiós.

LESSON 14

AT THE STORE

Helen—Good day, sir.
Shopkeeper—What do you wish?
Helen—I want two bottles of milk, five pounds of sugar and white bread.
Shopkeeper—Here's the milk, the sugar and the white bread. Do you wish anything more?
Helen—I'm going to read my list. Oh yes, I want two jars of jelly.
Shopkeeper—What flavor?
Helen—One jar of grape and one of strawberry.
Shopkeeper—Do you want a large or small jar?
Helen—Is there a medium jar?
Shopkeeper—Yes, there is a medium jar.
Helen—Then a medium jar, please.
Shopkeeper—Is that all?
Helen—Yes, I think so. Here are ten dollars.
Shopkeeper—Thank you very much. Here is the change. Good-by. Good day.
Helen—You're welcome, sir. Good-by.
Shopkeeper—And you, child, what do you wish?
Susan—Nothing, sir. I'm with Helen.
Shopkeeper—And *you*, young man, what do *you* wish?
Robert—Nothing, sir. I'm with Helen.
Shopkeeper—Good day, children. Pay attention to the lights. Go only if the light is green.
All the children—Yes, sir. Good-by.

WORD STUDY

oreja (la)

tienda (la)

leche (la)

galleta (la)

LECCIÓN 15

EN LA PASTELERÍA

Do you like to look into shop windows? Everybody does, and especially when the window is full of delicious cakes and cookies. Robert, Helen and their friends are no exceptions.

Elena—Vamos a la pastelería.
Susana—Mmm. Hay cosas deliciosas aquí.
Elena—¿Cuáles galletas te gustan, Roberto?
Roberto—¿Cuáles? ¡Todas! Elena, es como la canción:

   Me gustan todas
   Me gustan todas
   Me gustan todas en general
   Pero éstas grandes
   Pero éstas grandes
   Pero éstas grandes, me gustan más.

Elena—Vamos a entrar. Tengo que regresar a casa pronto.

Tendera—Buenas tardes, niña. ¿Qué deseas?
Elena—Un bizcocho de chocolate y una libra de galletas.

Tendera—¿Deseas el bizcocho grande o el pequeño?
Elena—Grande, por favor. ¿Cuánto cuesta?
Tendera—Dos dólares.
Elena—Está bien. Y las galletas, por favor.
Tendera—¿Cuáles galletas?
Elena—Éstas grandes de la vitrina.
Tendera—¿Deseas algo más?
Elena—No señora, muchas gracias.
Tendera—Toma, niña. Cuatro galletas para tí y para tus amigos.

Todos—Muchas gracias, señora. Adiós.
Tendera—Adiós, niños.

LESSON 15

THE PASTRY SHOP

Helen—Let's go to the pastry shop.
Susan—Mmm. There are delicious things there.
Helen—Which cookies do you like, Robert?
Robert—Which? All of them. Helen, it's like the song:

> I like them all.
> I like them all.
> I like them all in general.
> But these big ones
> But these big ones
> But these big ones, I prefer.

Helen—Let's go in. I have to return home soon.
Shopkeeper—Good afternoon, children. What do you wish?
Helen—A chocolate cake and a pound of cookies.
Shopkeeper—Do you want the large or the small one?
Helen—The large one, please. How much is it?
Shopkeeper—Two dollars.
Helen—That's fine. And the cookies, please.
Shopkeeper—Which cookies?
Helen—The big ones in the window.
Shopkeeper—Do you wish anything else?
Helen—No thanks, ma'am.
Shopkeeper—Here you are, [child]. Four cookies for you and for your friends.
All the children—Thank you very much, ma'am. Good-by.
Shopkeeper—Good-by, children.

QUIZ 5

Shall we try another game of *Sí* or *No*? Say *Sí* if the sentence is correct, and repeat the sentence. Remember to give the correct answer if you think the sentence is not true. Then turn to page 44 to see if you're right.

1. La mamá quiere un bizcocho de chocolate.
2. Elena va a comprar les galletas en la tienda de comestibles.
3. Elena desea un tarro grande.
4. El bizcocho cuesta cinco dólares.

LECCIÓN 16

SÓLO UN JUEGO, MAMÁ

Helen likes number games so well that she makes her mother play "just one," even though someone is coming to visit soon.

Elena—Mamá, mamá. Aquí estamos.
Mamá—Gracias, niños. ¿Traes todo, Elena?
Elena—Creo que sí, mamá. Roberto trae cinco libras de azúcar, dos botellas de leche, pan blanco, y dos tarros de jalea, un tarro de uvas y uno de fresa.
Mamá—Muchas gracias, Roberto. ¿Tienes la vuelta, Elena?

Elena—Sí. Aquí está.
Mamá—Entonces, niños—todos a la cocina. El chocolate está en los vasos.
Elena—Mamá, las galletas.
Mamá—Sí, ¡cómo no! Vamos a comer galletas también.
Elena—Mamá, ¿qué hora es?
Mamá—Son las dos.
Elena—¿A qué hora viene tu amiga?

Mamá—Viene a las cuatro y media. ¿Por qué?
Elena—¿Hay tiempo para jugar un poco, mamá?
Mamá—No hay tiempo, Elena.
Elena—Sólo un poco, mamá, por favor.
Mamá—Está bien. ¿A cuál juego quieres jugar?
Elena—El juego de "Lo Tengo" con los números. Mamá, por favor explícales el juego a mis amigos.
Mamá—Con much gusto. El juego es muy fácil si saben los números. Elena sabe los números del uno al diez.
Roberto—Señora, yo sé los números del diez al veinte. Escucha: once, doce, trece, catorce, quince, diez y seis, diez y siete, diez y ocho, diez y nueve, veinte.
Todos—Muy bien, Roberto.

LESSON 16

ONLY PLAY ONE, MOTHER

Helen—Mother, Mother. Here we are.
Mother—Thank you, children. Do you have everything, Helen?
Helen—I think so, Mama. Robert has five pounds of sugar, two bottles of milk, white bread and two jars of jelly, one jar of grape and one of strawberry.
Mother—Thank you very much, Robert. Do you have the change, Helen?
Helen—Yes. Here it is.
Mother—Then, children, everyone to the kitchen. The chocolate is in the glasses.
Helen—Mama, the cookies.
Mother—Yes, of course. We are going to eat the cookies also.
Helen—Mama, what time is it?
Mother—It's two o'clock.
Helen—What time is your friend coming?
Mother—She's coming at four-thirty. Why?
Helen—We have time to play a little, Mother?
Mother—There is no time, Helen.
Helen—Only a little one, Mother, please.
Mother—All right. Which game do you want to play?
Helen—The game "I Have It" (Bingo) with the numbers. Mother, please explain the game to my friends.
Mother—With pleasure. The game is very easy if you know the numbers. Helen knows the numbers from one to ten.
Robert—Ma'am, I know the numbers from ten to twenty—Listen: eleven, twelve, thirteen, fourteen, fifteen, sixteen, seventeen, eighteen, nineteen, twenty.
All the children—Very good, Robert.

ANSWERS TO QUIZ 5

1. *Sí.* La mamá quiere un bizcocho de chocolate.
2. *No.* Elena va a comprar las galletas en la pastelería.
3. *No.* Elena desea un tarro mediano.
4. *No.* El bizcocho cuesta dos dólares.

LECCIÓN 17

¡LO TENGO!

Games, like fairy tales, are the same in many parts of the world. Would you like to learn the Spanish way of playing Bingo?

Susana—¿Cómo se llama el juego, Elena?

Elena—Se llama "Lo Tengo." Mamá va a explicarlo todo.

Mamá—Sí, pero primero vamos a aprender los números hasta cincuenta.

Elena—No, mamá, es difícil. No hay tiempo. Vamos a jugar hasta veinte.

Mamá—No, Elena. Los números hasta cincuenta son muy fáciles. Escucha. Veinte, veinte y uno, veinte y dos.

Elena—¡Es fácil! Tienes razón, mamá. Yo puedo continuar. Escucha. Veinte y tres, veinte y cuatro.

Mamá—Está bien. Entonces treinta, treinta y uno, cuarenta, cuarenta y uno, cincuenta, cincuenta y uno. Entonces vamos a repetir: veinte, treinta, cuarenta, cincuenta.

Todos—Veinte, treinta, cuarenta, cincuenta.

Mamá—Muy bien. Y ahora, tomen el papel. Dibujen cinco líneas *así* y cinco líneas *así*.

Encantada, señora

Mamá—Ahora, escriban A encima de la columna número uno; escriban E encima de la columna número dos; escriban I encima de la columna número tres; escriban O encima de la columna número cuatro.

Mamá—Ahora escriban cualquier número del uno al cincuenta en cada cuadrado.

Mamá—Aquí tienen muchos pedazos de papel. Si yo digo un número y ustedes lo tienen, cubran el número con un papel. Cuando todos los números de una línea estén cubiertos, griten, "Lo tengo."

Mamá—"A" cuatro, "A" ocho, "E" diez y seis, "I" veinte y cuatro, "O" cuarenta, "I" treinta y dos, "O" cuarenta y nueve, "I" veinte y ocho, "E" once, "E" quince . . .

Susana—Lo Tengo, Lo Tengo.

Elena—Vamos a ver.

Todos—¡Qué suerte!

Mamá—Sí, Susana lo tiene. Vamos a darle un premio a Susana. Tres galletas. Pues, niños, adiós. Hasta mañana.

Todos—Hasta mañana, señora. Gracias.

LESSON 17

I HAVE IT!

Susan—What's the game called, Helen?

Helen—It's called "I Have it," (Bingo). Mother is going to explain everything to you.

Mother—Yes, but first we are going to learn the numbers to fifty.

Helen—No, Mother, it's difficult. There's no time. Let's play to twenty.

Mother—No, Helen. The numbers to fifty are very easy. Listen: twenty, twenty-one, twenty-two.

Helen—It is easy! You're right, Mother, I can continue. Listen: twenty-three, twenty-four.

Mother—That's good. Then thirty, thirty-one, forty, forty-one, fifty, fifty-one. Then let's repeat twenty, thirty, forty, fifty.

All the children—twenty, thirty, forty, fifty.

Mother—Very good. And now take the paper. Draw five lines this way and five lines this way.

Helen—Yes, Mother.

Mother—Now write "A" above column number one, "E" above column number two, "I" above column number three, "O" above number four. Now write any number from one to fifty in each square. Here are many pieces of paper. If I call a number that you have, cover it with a paper. When all the numbers in one line are covered, yell "I Have It."

"A" four, "A" eight, "E" sixteen, "I" twenty-four, "O" forty, "I" thirty-two, "O" forty-nine, "I" twenty-eight, "E" eleven, "E" fifteen.

Susan—I have it, I have it!

Helen—Let's see.

All the children—What luck!

Mother—Yes, Susan has it. Let's give the prize to Susan. Three cookies. Well, children, good-by. Until tomorrow.

All the children—Until tomorrow, ma'am. Thank you.

WORD STUDY

jalea (la)

azúcar (el)

pastelería (la)

bizcocho (el)

46

LECCIÓN 18

ENCANTADA, SEÑORA

Do you make your mother feel very proud of you when company comes? Make her even prouder by learning how to greet her visitors in another language.

Mamá—Felisa, bienvenida, bienvenida a mi casa.

La señora Alvarez—Gracias, Clara.

Mamá—Pasa, pasa. Quiero presentarte a mi familia. Ésta es mi hija Elena. Elena, ésta es mi amiga de la escuela, la señora Alvarez.

Elena—Encantada, señora.

La señora Alvarez—Encantada, Elena. ¡Qué niña tan bonita! ¿Cuántos años tienes, Elena?

Elena—Tengo ocho años, señora.

Mamá—Felisa, ven aquí. Éste es mi hijo, Carlitos.

La señora Alvarez—Encantada, Carlitos.

La señora Alvarez—Creo que Carlitos tiene miedo de mí.

Elena—No, señora. No se apure. No tiene miedo de usted. Llora siempre.

La señora Alvarez—¿Cuántos años tiene tu hermanito?

Elena—Tiene dos años, señora.

La señora Alvarez—¿Dónde está tu esposo, Clara?

Mamá—Carlos está en la oficina. Regresa siempre a las seis. Carlos quiere verte, Felisa. Come aquí con nosotros esta tarde.

La señora Alvarez—Con mucho gusto.

Mamá—Siéntate, Felisa. Voy a preparar una merienda. Elena, ¿por qué no enseñas la casa a la señora Alvarez? Ve. Enseña tu cuarto a la señora.

Elena—Con mucho gusto, mamá.

¿Quieres recitar conmigo?

A E I O U
Arbolito del Perú
Yo tengo ocho años
¿Cuántos años tienes tú?

LESSON 18

DELIGHTED, MADAM

Mother—Felicia, welcome, welcome to my house.
Mrs. Alvarez—Thank you, Clara.
Mother—Come in, come in. I want to introduce you to my family. This is my daughter, Helen. Helen, this is a schoolmate, Mrs. Alvarez.
Helen—Very pleased to meet you.
Mrs. Alvarez—Delighted, Helen. What a beautiful child! How old are you, Helen?
Helen—I am eight years old, ma'am.
Mother—Felicia, come here. This is my son, Charles.
Mrs. Alvarez—Delighted, Charles. I believe that Charles is afraid of me.
Helen—No, ma'am, don't worry. He's not afraid of you. He always cries.
Mrs. Alvarez—How old is your little brother?
Helen—He's two years old, ma'am.
Mrs. Alvarez—Where is your husband, Clara?
Mother—Charles is at the office. He always returns at six o'clock.
Charles wants to see you, Felicia. Dine here with us this evening.
Mrs. Alvarez—With much pleasure.
Mother—Sit down, Felicia: I'm going to prepare a snack. Helen, why don't you show the house to Mrs. Alvarez? Go show your room to the lady.
Helen—With much pleasure, Mother.

Would you like to recite with me?

AEIOU
Little tree of Peru
I am eight years old
How old are you?

QUIZ 6

Can you answer these questions in Spanish?
1. ¿Cómo se llama el juego?
2. ¿Cómo se llama la amiga?
3. ¿A qué hora regresa el papá de Elena?
4. ¿Cuántos años tiene Elena?

Turn to page 51 to see if you have answered correctly.

LECCIÓN 19

ME GUSTA TODO

Helen takes the visitor on a tour of the house. In which room do you think they spend the most time? Let's see if you've guessed correctly.

La señora Alvarez—Vamos a ver la casa, Elena.
Elena—¿Quiere usted empezar con mi dormitorio, señora?
La señora Alvarez—Sí, ¿cómo no, Elena?
Elena—Aquí está, señora.
La señora Alvarez—¡Qué dormitorio tan bonito, Elena! Me gusta el color. Me gustan los muebles también.
Elena—Muchas gracias, señora.
La señora Alvarez—¿Y qué veo aquí? Una cuna con dos muñecas.

Elena—¿Le gustan mis muñecas?
La señora Alvarez—Me gustan mucho. ¿Cómo se llama esta rubia?
Elena—Se llama Marta.

La señora Alvarez—¿Y cómo se llama esta morena?
Elena—Se llama Rosita.
La señora Alvarez—¿Qué hay en esta caja, Elena?
Elena—Los trajes de mis muñecas, señora. Aquí hay un traje azul, un traje amarillo y un traje rojo. ¿Vamos a ver los otros cuartos ahora, señora?
La señora Alvarez—Sí. Con mucho gusto.
Elena—Éste es el dormitorio de mi hermanito.

La señora Alvarez—¿Dónde está el dormitorio de tus padres?
Elena—Aquí está. Los muebles son nuevos. ¿Le gustan?

(continued)

LECCIÓN 19

La señora Alvarez—Sí. Me gustan mucho.
Elena—Vamos al comedor ahora.
La señora Alvarez—¡Qué cuarto tan grande! ¡Qué mesa tan grande también!

Elena—La cocina está aquí.
Mamá—Felisa, Elena, la merienda está lista. Aquí en la sala.
La señora Alvarez—Clara, tienes una casa preciosa. Te felicito.
Mamá—Muchas gracias, Felisa. Siéntate aquí y vamos a comer el bizcocho de chocolate. Elena no puede esperar más.

Vamos a cantar:

Fray Carlito, Fray Carlito,
¿Duermes tú? ¿Duermes tú?
Toca la campana
Toca la campana
Din din don
Din din don.

LESSON 19

I LIKE EVERYTHING

Mrs. Alvarez—Let's see the house, Helen.
Helen—Do you want to start with my bedroom, ma'am?
Mrs. Alvarez—Yes, of course, Helen.
Helen—Here it is, ma'am.
Mrs. Alvarez—What a beautiful bedroom, Helen! I like the color. I also like the furniture.
Helen—Thank you very much, ma'am.
Mrs. Alvarez—And what do I see here? A cradle with two dolls!
Helen—Do you like my dolls?
Mrs. Alvarez—I like them very much. What's the name of this blonde one?
Helen—Her name is Martha.
Mrs. Alvarez—And what's the name of this brunette one?
Helen—Her name is Rosita.
Mrs. Alvarez—What's in this box, Helen?
Helen—My dolls' clothes, ma'am. Here is a blue dress, a yellow dress and a red dress. Shall we go see the other rooms now, ma'am?
Mrs. Alvarez—Yes, with much pleasure.
Helen—This is my little brother's bedroom.
Mrs. Alvarez—Where is your parents' bedroom?
Helen—Here it is. The furniture is new. Do you like it?

(continued)

ANSWERS TO QUIZ 6

1. Se llama "Lo Tengo."
2. Se llama la señora Alvarez.
3. Regresa a las seis.
4. Tiene ocho años.

LESSON 19

Mrs. Alvarez—Yes, I like it very much.
Helen—Let's go to the dining room now.
Mrs. Alvarez—What a big room! What a big table, too.
Helen—The kitchen is here.
Mother—Felicia, Helen, the snack is ready. Here, in the living room.
Mrs. Alvarez—Clara, you have a lovely house. Congratulations.
Mother—Thank you very much, Felicia. Sit down here and let's eat the chocolate cake. Helen can't wait any longer.

Let's Sing!

Brother Charles, Brother Charles
Are you sleeping, Are you sleeping,
Morning bells are ringing
Morning bells are ringing
Ding, Ding Dong
Ding, Ding Dong

WORD STUDY

oficina (la)

pan (el)

juego (el)

vaso (el)

cincuenta

escuela (la)

LECCIÓN 20

¿AYUDAS A TU MAMÁ?

A "company" table takes a little longer time to set, but it does look pretty and doesn't it seem to make the food taste better?

La señora Alvarez—Tocas el piano muy bien, Elena. Me gusta mucho "El Jarabe Tapatío."

Elena—Gracias, señora.

Mamá—Ahora, hazme el favor de poner la mesa.

La señora Alvarez—¿Sabe Elena poner la mesa?

Mamá—Sí, como no. Elena sabe hacer muchas cosas.

Elena—Perdóname, mamá. ¿Dónde está el mantel? ¿Dónde están las servilletas?

Mamá—El mantel y las servilletas están en el aparador del comedor.

Elena—Perdóname, mamá. ¿Qué platos y cubiertos uso?

Mamá—Usa los platos y los cubiertos que hay en el aparador.

Elena—Vamos a ver. Primero pongo el mantel y las servilletas. Ahora pongo los platos. Perdóname, mamá. ¿Cuántos platos pongo?

Mamá—Cuatro. Esta tarde tú vas a comer en la mesa grande, con nosotros.

Elena—¡Qué bueno, mamá! Gracias.

Elena—Vamos a ver. Pongo un tenedor, un cuchillo, una cuchara grande y una cucharita con cada plato. Pongo las flores en el centro con el salero y el pimentero. Pongo los candeleros a cada lado. ¡Qué lindo! Mamá, ven a ver.

Mamá—Muy lindo, Elena. Pero, ¿dónde están los vasos?

Elena—Ay, mamá, tienes razón. Perdóname. ¿Qué vasos uso?

Mamá—Usa los vasos que hay en el aparador también.

Elena—Mamá, ven a ver ahora.

Mamá—Ahora sí. ¡Qué sorpresa tan buena para papá!

Vamos a cantar:

San Serení de la buena, buena vida
Hacen así
Así las camareras
Así, así, así . . .
¡Así me gusta a mí!

LESSON 20

DO YOU HELP YOUR MOTHER?

Mrs. Alvarez—You play the piano very well, Helen. I like "El Jarabe Tapatío," very much.

Helen—Thank you very much, ma'am.

Mother—Now please set the table.

Mrs. Alvarez—Does Helen know how to set the table?

Mother—Yes, of course. Helen knows how to do many things.

Helen—Pardon me, Mother. Where is the table cloth? Where are the napkins?

Mother—The table cloth and the napkins are in the buffet in the dining room.

Helen—Pardon me, Mother. Which plates and silverware shall I use?

Mother—Use the plates and silverware in the buffet.

Helen—Let's see. First I put on the tablecloth and the napkins. Now I put on the plates. Pardon me, Mother. How many plates do I put on?

Mother—Four. This evening you are going to eat at the big table with us.

Helen—How nice, Mother. Thanks.

Helen—Let's see. I place a fork, a knife, a tablespoon and a tea-spoon with each plate. I place the flowers in the center with the salt shaker and the pepper shaker. I place the candlesticks at each side. How pretty. Mother, come and see.

Mother—Very pretty, Helen. But where are the glasses?

Helen—Mother, you're right. I'm sorry. Which glasses shall I use?

Mother—Use the glasses that are in the buffet, also.

Helen—Mother, come and see now.

Mother—Now it's fine. What a nice surprise for Father.

Let's Sing!
Saint Serini of the good, good life
The waitresses do this,
Like this, like this, like this.
I like it like this.

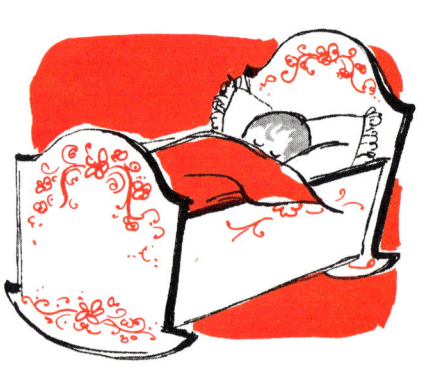

WORD STUDY

cuna (la)

muebles (los)

muñeca (la)

LECCIÓN 21

¡QUÉ COMIDA TAN RICA!

Good table manners are so important. Even when you don't really like certain foods, it's nice to refuse them politely. Let's find out how Spanish-speaking children do it.

Elena—Mamá, mamá, es papá. Buenas tardes, papacito. ¿Estás cansado?

Papá—Un poco cansado, sí. ¿Dónde está tu mamá?

Elena—Está en la sala con la señora Alvarez.

Papá—Ah, sí.

Mamá—Carlos, ven aquí a la sala.

Mamá—Siéntate aquí, Felisa. Tú, Elena, siéntate aquí.

La señora Alvarez—¡Qué comida tan rica! El arroz con pollo está delicioso. Pásame las habichuelas. Están muy buenas.

Papá—Felisa, encantado de verte.

La señora Alvarez—Yo también, Carlos. Encantada de verte. ¿Cómo estás?

Papá—Un poco cansado pero estoy bien. Perdóname. Voy a ver a Carlitos.

Mamá—Prepárate, Carlos. Vamos a comer en seguida.

Mamá— . . . ¿Un poco más de ensalada, Felisa?

La señora Alvarez—Sí, gracias . . . ¿Un poco más para tí, Carlos?

Papá—Sí, gracias. ¿Un poco para tí, Elena?

Elena—No, gracias, papá. Quiero esperar el postre.

Papá—¿Qué hay de postre?

Mamá—No es nada. Un flan de frutas.

Papá—¡Qué bueno! Me gusta mucho el flan.

La señora Alvarez—Y el flan de frutas es mi postre favorito.

Mamá—Vamos a tomar el café en el salón. Elena, ¿quieres mirar la televisión en tu cuarto?

Elena—Oh, sí, mamacita. Con su permiso, señora Alvarez. Con tu permiso, papá.

LESSON 21

WHAT A DELICIOUS MEAL!

Helen—Mother, Mother. Here's Father. Good afternoon, Father. Are you tired?

Father—A little tired, yes. Where is Mother?

Helen—She's in the living room with Mrs. Alvarez.

Father—Ah yes.

Mother—Charles, come here to the living room.

Father—Felicia, delighted to see you.

Mrs. Alvarez—So am I, Charles. Delighted to see you. How are you?

Father—A little tired, but I'm well. Excuse me. I am going to see Charlie.

Mother—Get ready, Charles. We are going to eat right away. The meal is ready.

Mother—Sit here, Felicia. You, Helen, sit here.

Mrs. Alvarez—What a delicious meal. The chicken with rice is delicious. Pass me the beans. They are very good.

Mother—A little more salad, Felicia?

Mrs. Alvarez—Yes, thank you. A little more for you, Charles?

Father—Yes, thank you. A little for you, Helen?

Helen—No thank you, Father. I want to wait for the dessert.

Father—What is there for dessert?

Mother—It's nothing. A custard with fruit.

Father—How nice. I like custard very much.

Mrs. Alvarez—And custard with fruit is my favorite dessert.

Mother—Let's have the coffee in the living room. Helen, do you want to watch television in your room?

Helen—Oh yes, Mother dear. Excuse me, Mrs. Alvarez. Excuse me, Father.

WORD STUDY

cocina (la)

tenedor (el)

merienda (la)

poner la mesa

plato (el)

mantel (el)

LECCIÓN 22

¿EN QUÉ CANAL?

It's important to know how to use the telephone. Don't you think so? Helen thinks the telephone is especially useful when she wants to find out which channel has the television program that she would like to see.

Elena—Perdóname, mamá. ¿Puedo usar el teléfono? Voy a telefonear a Roberto. Hay un programa especial en la televisión, pero no sé la hora. Roberto sabe las horas de todos los programas.
Mamá—Usa el teléfono de mi dormitorio.
Elena—Gracias, mamá.
Elena—Señorita, deme el número de teléfono de Roberto Pérez, por favor. Vive en la calle de León, en el número ocho.
 Ocho-cinco, dos, cuatro, nueve . . . Muchas gracias, señorita.

Elena—Bueno.
 ¿Quién habla? Señora Pérez, ¿está Roberto en casa?
 Muchas gracias, espero.
 ¿Roberto? Habla Elena.
 Bien, gracias. Roberto, por favor, ¿en qué canal está el programa de títeres?
 ¿En el canal cuatro?
 ¿A qué hora?
 ¿Ahora mismo? Gracias, voy en seguida. Hasta mañana.
Elena—¡Qué programa tan maravilloso, mamá! Una señora con títeres—y trajes ricos—y un baile lindo, Las Chiapanecas. Ya tengo sueño, mamá.
Mamá—Vete a dormir. Dales las "Buenas noches" a la señora Alvarez y a papá.
Elena—Buenas noches, señora.
La señora Alvarez—Buenas noches, Elena. Dame un beso.
Elena—Buena noches, papá.
Papá—Buenas noches, Elena. ¿Tienes un beso para papá?
Elena—Buenas noches, mamá.
Mamá—Buenas noches, Elena, y muchas gracias.

Vamos a cantar:

Ay Chiapanecas, ay ay
Ay Chiapanecas, ay ay
Ay Chiapanecas, ay ay
Ay Chiapanecas, ay ay.

LESSON 22

ON WHAT CHANNEL?

Helen—Pardon me, Mother. May I use the telephone? I want to call Robert. There is a special program on television, but I don't know the time. Robert knows the time of all the programs.
Mother—Use the telephone in my bedroom.
Helen—Thank you, Mother.
   Miss, please give me the telephone number of Robert Perez. He lives on Leon Street at number eight.
   Eight-five, two, four, nine. . . . Thank you very much, miss.
   Hello.
   Who's speaking? Mrs. Perez, is Robert at home?
   Thank you very much. I'll wait.
   Robert, Helen speaking.
   Well, thank you, Robert. On what channel is the puppet program, please?
   On channel four? At what time?
   Right now? Thank you, I'm going. See you tomorrow.
Helen—What a marvelous program, Mother! A woman with puppets. And lovely clothes, a nice dance, Girls of Chiapas. I'm sleepy now, Mother.
Mother—Go to sleep. Say "good night" to Mrs. Alvarez and to Father.
Helen—Good night, ma'am.
Mrs. Alvarez—Good night, Helen. Give me a kiss.
Helen—Good night, Father.
Father—Good night, Helen. Do you have a kiss for Father?
Helen—Good night, Mother.
Mother—Good night, Helen, and thank you very much.

Let's Sing!

Ay, Girls of Chiapas, ay, ay
Ay, girls of Chiapas, ay, ay
Ay, girls of Chiapas, ay, ay
Ay, girls of Chiapas, ay ay.

QUIZ 7

Now we will play another drawing game. After each of the next four Spanish words, make a drawing of the thing each means to you. Then turn to the page in the dictionary shown beside the words in the manual and see if you can find the drawing and Spanish words.

1. Dibuja una *mesa*.
   (*See dictionary page* 30)

2. Dibuja un *plato*.
   (*See dictionary page* 37)

3. Dibuja una *flor*.
   (*See dictionary page* 21)

4. Dibuja un *títere*.
   (*See dictionary page* 44)

LECCIÓN 23

VAMOS A JUGAR A LA ESCUELA

Playing school is another favorite game of children everywhere. Do you think you'd like Robert as your teacher?

Elena—Hola, ¿qué tal? Mamá, ¿pueden entrar Juana, Susana, Rosa, Roberto y José?
Elena—¿Podemos jugar en la casa?
Mamá—Con mucho gusto. ¿Por qué no se van todos al cuarto de Elena?

Rosa—¿A qué vamos a jugar?
Susana—¿Con las muñecas de Elena?
Roberto y José—¡Oh, no!
Rosa—Ya sé. Vamos a jugar a la escuela.
Juana y Susana—¡Buena idea!
Juana—Roberto hace de maestro.
Susana—Sí, Roberto hace de maestro.
Roberto—Vamos a empezar. Buenos días, niños.
Todos—Buenos días, señor.
Roberto—¿Quién puede recitar los números del uno al diez?
Todos—Yo, yo.
Roberto—Empieza, Susana, por favor.
Susana—Uno, dos, tres, cuatro, cinco.

Roberto—Continúa, José, por favor.
José—Seis, siete, ocho, nueve, diez.
Roberto—Muy bien. Vamos a jugar a "Lo Tengo" con los números. ¿Estan listos? A cuatro, E catorce, I diez, Y seis, A nueve, O viente y ocho.
Juana—"Lo Tengo."
José—¿Ya?
Roberto—Sí, Juana tiene todos los numeros. Ahora vamos a aprender los días de la semana. Perdóneme . . . Señora Sánchez.
Señora Sánchez—por favor, escriba los días de la semana aquí.
Roberto—Miren el calendario. Los días de la semana son: lunes, martes, miércoles, jueves, viernes, sábado y domingo. Repitan.
Todos—Lunes, martes, miércoles, jueves, viernes, sábado, domingo.
Roberto—Muy bien. Hay un poema fácil con los días de la semana. Escuchen:

Lunes, martes, miércoles, tres,
Jueves, viernes, sábado, seis,
Y domingo siete.

Mamá—Elena, niños. Continúen más tarde. Ahora pasen a la cocina a tomar chocolate y . . . galletas.
Todos—Galletas . . . Mmm. Con mucho gusto, señora.

LESSON 23

LET'S PLAY SCHOOL

Helen—Hello. How are you?
  Mother, may Joan, Susan, Rose, Robert and Joseph come in? May we play in the house?
Mother—Gladly, of course. Why don't you all go to Helen's room?
Rose—What are we going to play?
Susan—With Helen's dolls?
Robert } Oh, no.
Joseph }
Rose—I know. Let's play school.
Joan   } Good idea.
Susan }
Joan—Robert will act as teacher.
Susan—Yes, Robert will act as teacher.
Robert—Let's begin. Good day, children.
All the children—Good day, sir.
Robert—Who can recite the numbers from one to ten?
All—Me, me.
Robert—Begin, Susan, please.
Susan—One, two, three, four, five.
Robert—Continue, Joseph, please.
Joseph—Six, seven, eight, nine, ten.
Robert—Very good. Let's play "I have it" (Bingo) with the numbers. Are you ready? "A" four, "E" fourteen, "I" ten, "Y" six, "A" nine, "O" twenty-eight.
Joan—I have it. Bingo.
Joseph—Already?
Robert—Yes, Joan has all the numbers. Now we are going to learn the days of the week. Excuse me, Mrs. Sanchez. Mrs. Sanchez, please write the days of the week here.
Robert—Look at the calendar. The days of the week are: Monday, Tuesday, Wednesday, Thursday, Friday, Saturday, Sunday. Repeat.
All the children—Monday, Tuesday, Wednesday, Thursday, Friday, Saturday, Sunday.
Robert—Very good. Here is an easy poem with the days of the week.

Monday, Tuesday, Wednesday, three
Thursday, Friday, Saturday, six
and Sunday, seven.

Mother—Helen, children, continue later. Now come to the kitchen for chocolate and cookies.
All—Cookies, mmm. Gladly, ma'am.

WORD STUDY

cuchillo (el)   **flor (la)**   **salón (el)**

LECCIÓN 24

¿CÓMO SE DICE?

Only one thing can take our friends away from the game they're playing. Can you guess what that might be?

Roberto—Silencio ahora, por favor. ¿Quién puede recitar el poema con los días de la semana?
José—Yo, señor.
Roberto—Recitar, por favor, José.
José—Lunes, martes, miércoles, tres,
   Jueves, viernes, sábado, seis,
   Y domingo siete.
Roberto—Muy bien, José.
Rosa—Vamos a aprender un poco de inglés. ¿Tú sabes inglés, Roberto?
Roberto—Muy bien. Repitan mi pregunta y la respuesta. ¿Cómo se dice "pluma" en inglés?
Todos—¿Cómo se dice "pluma" en inglés?
Roberto—Se dice "pen."
Todos—Se dice "pen."

Roberto—¿Cómo se dice "pizarra" en inglés?
Todos—¿Cómo se dice "pizarra" en inglés?
Roberto—Se dice "blackboard."
Todos—Se dice "blackboard."
Roberto—Muy bien. Y ahora vamos a dibujar. Aquí hay papel y creyones.

José—Yo quiero el creyón azul.
Juana—Yo quiero el creyón rojo.
Roberto—Silencio. Toma, Susana: un creyón verde; un creyón azul; un creyón rojo, y un creyón amarillo. Toma, José—Juana—Rosa.
José—¿Qué vamos a dibujar?
Rosa—Ya sé. Una escuela.
Susana—No.
Juana—Ya sé. Una casa.
Roberto—¡Buena idea! Cada uno dibuja su casa. Primero, el interior.

Roberto—Muéstranos tu dibujo, Rosa . . . ¿Qué es ésto?
Rosa—Es la sala.
Roberto—¿Qué es esto?
Rosa—Es el cuarto de baño.
Roberto—Muy bien.

Mamá—¡Qué casas tan lindos! Hay un cuento muy bueno con casas y con.
Todos—Por favor, señora, el cuento, el cuento.
Mamá—Pues bien. Es el cuento de Los Tres Cerpitos.

61

LESSON 24

HOW DO YOU SAY — ?

Robert—Silence now, please. Who can recite the poem of the days of the week?
Joseph—I, sir.
Robert—Recite, please, Joseph.
Joseph—Monday, Tuesday, Wednesday, three
Thursday, Friday, Saturday, six
And Sunday, seven.
Robert—Very good, Joseph.
Rose—Let's learn some English. Do you know English, Robert?
Robert—Very well. Repeat my question and the answer. How do you say "pluma" in English?
All the children—How do you say "pluma" in English?
Robert—You say "pen."
All the children—You say "pen."
Robert—How do you say "pizarra" in English?
All the children—How do you say "pizarra" in English?
Robert—You say "blackboard."
All the children—You say "blackboard."
Robert—Very good, and now we're going to draw. Here are paper and crayons.
Joseph—I want the blue crayon.
Joan—I want the red crayon.
Robert—Silence. Susan, take a green crayon, a blue crayon, a red crayon and a yellow crayon. Here Joseph, Joan, Rose.
Joseph—What are we going to draw?
Rose—I know, a school.
Susan—No!
Joan—I know, a house.
Robert—Good idea. Each of you draw your house. The inside first. Show us your drawing, Rose. What's this?
Rose—It's the living room.
Robert—What's this?
Rose—It's the bathroom.
Robert—Very good.
Mother—What pretty houses! There's a good story with houses and with . . .
All—Please, ma'am, the story, the story.
Mother—Very well. It's the story of The Three Little Pigs.

QUIZ 8

Can you answer these questions in Spanish?
1. ¿Cuáles son los días de la semana?
2. ¿Cómo se dice "chalk" en español?
3. ¿Cómo se dice "yellow" en español?
4. ¿Cómo se dice "living room" en español?

Turn to page 64 to see if you have answered correctly.

LECCIÓN 25

LOS TRES CERDITOS

The story of The Three Pigs is a favorite everywhere. "I'll huff and I'll puff and I'll blow the house down" is a sentence that stays in our minds long after we've heard the story. Would you like to learn how it sounds in another language?

Mamá—Había una vez una casa en el bosque. En la casa viven la madre y tres hermanos. El hermano mayor es muy inteligente. Trabaja mucho. El segundo hermano es perezoso. Toca la flauta todo el día. El hermano menor es muy, muy perezoso. Toca el violín todo el día.

Un día el hermano mayor dice: "Mamá, te quiero mucho pero deseo ganarme la vida fuera de la casa." El segundo hermano dice: "Sí, mamá, te quiero mucho, pero deseo ganarme la vida fuera de la casa." El hermano menor dice: "Y yo, también."

La mamá está muy triste pero dice: "Bueno, si quieren ganarse la vida fuera, voy a preparar una canasta para cada uno con frutas, pan, y otras cosas buenas."

—"Gracias, mamá,"—dicen todos.

La mamá prepara las canastas con cosas buenas y le da una a cada uno.

—"Adiós, mamá,"—dice el hermano mayor.
—"Adiós, mamá,"—dice el segundo hermano.
—"Adiós, mamá," dice el hermano menor.
—"Adiós, hijos. Hasta pronto. Tengan cuidado en el bosque. Cuidado con los animales feroces."

Los hermanos empiezan a caminar por el bosque. El hermano mayor recuerda las palabras de su mamá y mira por todas partes. Sus dos hermanos se burlan de él:
—"Ja, ja, ja," dice el segundo hermano. "Tiene miedo a los animales feroces."—
"Ja, ja, ja," dice el hermano menor. "Tiene miedo a los animales. Yo estoy cansado. Voy a construir mi casa aquí."

—"No, no, no"—dice el hermano mayor.— "Aquí, no. Creo que hay un lobo muy cerca."

Juana—¿Hay un lobo, señora?

Mamá—Vamos a ver después. Ahora quiero saber si escuchan con atención. ¿Quién puede empezar el cuento?

Todos—Yo, yo.

Mamá—Roberto, por favor.

Roberto—Hay una casa en el bosque.

Elena—Hay tres hermanos.

José—Los hermanos quieren ganarse la vida fuera de la casa.

Juana—Dicen "Adiós" a su mamá.

Elena—La mamá dice: "Tengan cuidado en el bosque, mucho cuidado."

Mamá—Muy bien. Excelente. Veo que tengo un auditorio maravilloso.

LESSON 25

THE THREE LITTLE PIGS

Once upon a time there was a house in the forest. In the house live a mother and three brothers. The oldest brother is very intelligent. He works a lot. The second brother is lazy. He plays the flute all day. The youngest brother is very, very lazy. He plays the violin all day.

One day, the oldest brother says: "Mama, I love you very much, but I wish to earn my living outside of the house." The second brother says: "Yes, Mother. I love you very much, but I wish to earn my living outside of the house." The youngest brother says: "And me, too."

The mother is very unhappy, but she says: "Good, if you want to earn your living outside, I'm going to prepare a basket for each of you with fruits, bread and other good things."

"Thank you, Mama," all say.

The mother prepares the baskets with good things and gives one to each one.

"Good-by, Mother," says the oldest brother.

"Good-by, Mother," says the second brother.

"Good-by, Mother," says the youngest brother.

"Good-by, sons. See you soon. Be careful in the forest. Watch out for wild animals."

The brothers start walking through the forest. The oldest brother remembers the words of his mother and looks around everywhere. His two brothers make fun of him.

"Ha, ha, ha," says the second brother. "He's afraid of the wild animals."

"Ha, ha, ha," says the youngest brother. "He's afraid of the animals. I'm tired. I'm going to build my house here."

"No, no, no," says the oldest brother. "Not here. I think there's a wolf very near."

Joan—Is there a wolf, ma'am?
Mother—We'll see later. Now I want to know if you listen well. Who can start the story?
All the children—I, I.
Mother—Robert, please.
Robert—There's a house in the forest.
Helen—There are three brothers.
Joseph—The brothers want to earn a living outside of the house.
Joan—They say "good-by" to their mother.
Helen—The mother says: "Be careful in the forest. Watch out."
Mother—Very well. Excellent. I see that I have a wonderful audience.

ANSWERS TO QUIZ 8

1. Son lunes, martes, miércoles, jueves, viernes, sábado, domingo.
2. Se dice "tiza."
3. Se dice "amarillo."
4. Se dice "sala."

LECCIÓN 26

¿QUIÉN TIENE MIEDO AL MAL LOBO GRANDE?

Do you believe in the proverb, "He who laughs last laughs best"? Can you think now of two reasons why the "wise" brother thinks the proverb is a good one?

Todos—Continúe el cuento, señora, por favor.
Mamá—Bueno . . . Entonces el hermano menor decide construir su casa de paja. "De paja, no, por favor. Una casa de paja no es sólida," dice el hermano mayor. Pero su hermano se burla de él, y construye su casa de paja en un dos por tres.

El segundo hermano decide construir su casa cerca de la casa del hermano menor. El hermano mayor dice otra vez: "Por favor, aquí no, creo que hay un lobo muy cerca." Pero el segundo hermano se burla de él y dice: "¿Quién tiene miedo al lobo? Voy a construir mi casa de madera." El hermano mayor dice otra vez: "De madera, no, por favor. Una casa de madera no es sólida." Pero su hermano se burla de él y construye su casa de madera en un dos por tres.

El hermano mayor va más lejos. Decide construir su casa de ladrillos.

Al día siguiente, muy temprano, el mal lobo aparece. El hermano menor corre dentro de su casa de paja. El lobo grita: "Cerdito, cerdito, déjame entrar. Si no, soplo y resoplo y hago volar la casa."

—"Por nada del mundo!"—dice el cerdito en voz muy baja porque tiene mucho miedo.

Entonces el lobo sopla y resopla, y la casa de paja cae en pedazos. El cerdito corre a la casa del segundo hermano.

(continued)

LECCIÓN 26

—"¡Aprisa, aprisa! ¡Entremos en la casa. Los cerditos entran pronto en la casa de madera. Pronto aparece el lobo."
—"Cerditos, cerditos, déjenme entrar. Si no, soplo y resoplo y hago volar la casa."
—"¡Por nada del mundo!"—dicen los cerditos.
Entonces el lobo sopla y resopla, y la casa de madera cae en pedazos. Los cerditos corren a la casa del hermano mayor.
—"¡Socorro, socorro! ¡Viene el mal lobo! ¡Vámonos todos al bosque!"
—"No se apuren, muchachos. Vamos a esperar al lobo aquí."
—"¿Aquí? No. El lobo nos mata."
Y en pocos minutos aparece el lobo.
—"Cerditos, cerditos, déjenme entrar. Si no, soplo y resoplo y hago volar la casa."
—"¡Por nada del mundo!"—dicen los tres cerditos.

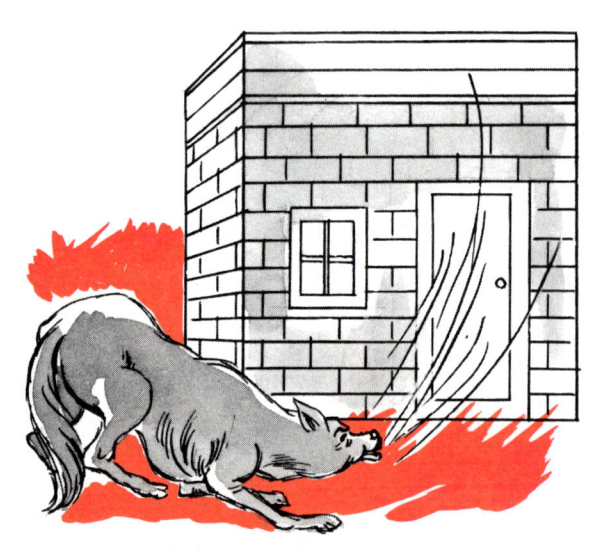

Entonces el lobo sopla y resopla, sopla y resopla, pero la casa de ladrillos no se cae. El lobo, furioso, se sube al techo. Decide entrar por la chimenea. Cuando el lobo entra por la chimenea, cae directamente en una caldera de agua hirviendo. Gritando de dolor, el lobo salta fuera y va corriendo por el bosque.

—"Gracias, hermano,"—dicen los dos cerditos.—"Tú siempre tienes razón."
Y los tres cerditos cantan:

"¿Quién tiene miedo al mal lobo grande,
Al mal lobo grande, al mal lobo grande?
¿Quién tiene miedo al mal lobo grande?
¿Yo? ¡Oh, no! ¡Oh, no!"

LESSON 26

WHO'S AFRAID OF THE BIG BAD WOLF?

All—Continue the story, madam please.

Mother—Very well. So the youngest brother decides to build his house of straw.

"Not of straw, please. A straw house is not solid," says the oldest brother.

But his brother makes fun of him and constructs his straw house in a jiffy.

The second brother decides to build his house near his younger brother's house.

Again, the oldest brother says, "Please, not here. I think there's a wolf very nearby."

But the second brother makes fun of him and says, "Who's afraid of the wolf? I'm going to build my house of wood."

Again, the oldest brother says, "Not of wood, please! A wooden house is not solid." But his brother makes fun of him and builds his house of wood in a jiffy.

The oldest brother goes farther away. He decides to build his house of bricks.

The following day, very early, the bad wolf appears. The youngest brother runs inside his straw house. The wolf growls "Little pig, little pig, let me in. If you don't, I'll huff and I'll puff and I'll blow your house in."

"For nothing in the world," says the little pig in a small voice because he's very much afraid.

So the wolf huffs and puffs, and the straw house falls to pieces. The little pig runs to the house of the second brother.

(continued)

WORD STUDY

habichuelas (las)

Tengo sueño.

traje (el)

ensalada (la)

maestra (la)

pluma (la)

LESSON 26

"Quickly, quickly, let me in the house."

The little pig enters the wooden house quickly. In a few minutes, the wolf appears. "Little pigs, little pigs, let me in. If you don't I'll huff and I'll puff and I'll blow your house in."

"For nothing in this world," say the two small pigs.

So the wolf huffs and he puffs and the wooden house falls to pieces. The little pigs run to the house of the oldest brother.

"Help! Help! The bad wolf is coming. Let's all go to the forest."

"Don't worry, brothers. Let's wait for the wolf here."

"Here? No. The wolf will kill us."

And in a few minutes, the wolf appears. "Little pigs, little pigs, let me enter. If you don't I'll huff and I'll puff and I'll blow the house in."

"For nothing in the world," say the three pigs.

So, the wolf huffs and puffs, he huffs and puffs, but the brick house does not fall.

The wolf, furious, climbs to the roof. He decides to enter through the chimney. When the wolf enters through the chimney he falls directly into a caldron of boiling water. Growling with pain, the wolf jumps out and goes racing through the forest.

"Thanks, brother," say the two little pigs. "You're always right."

And the three little pigs sing:

Who's afraid of the big bad wolf,
Of the big bad wolf, of the big bad wolf?
Who's afraid of the big bad wolf?
I? Oh no! Oh no!

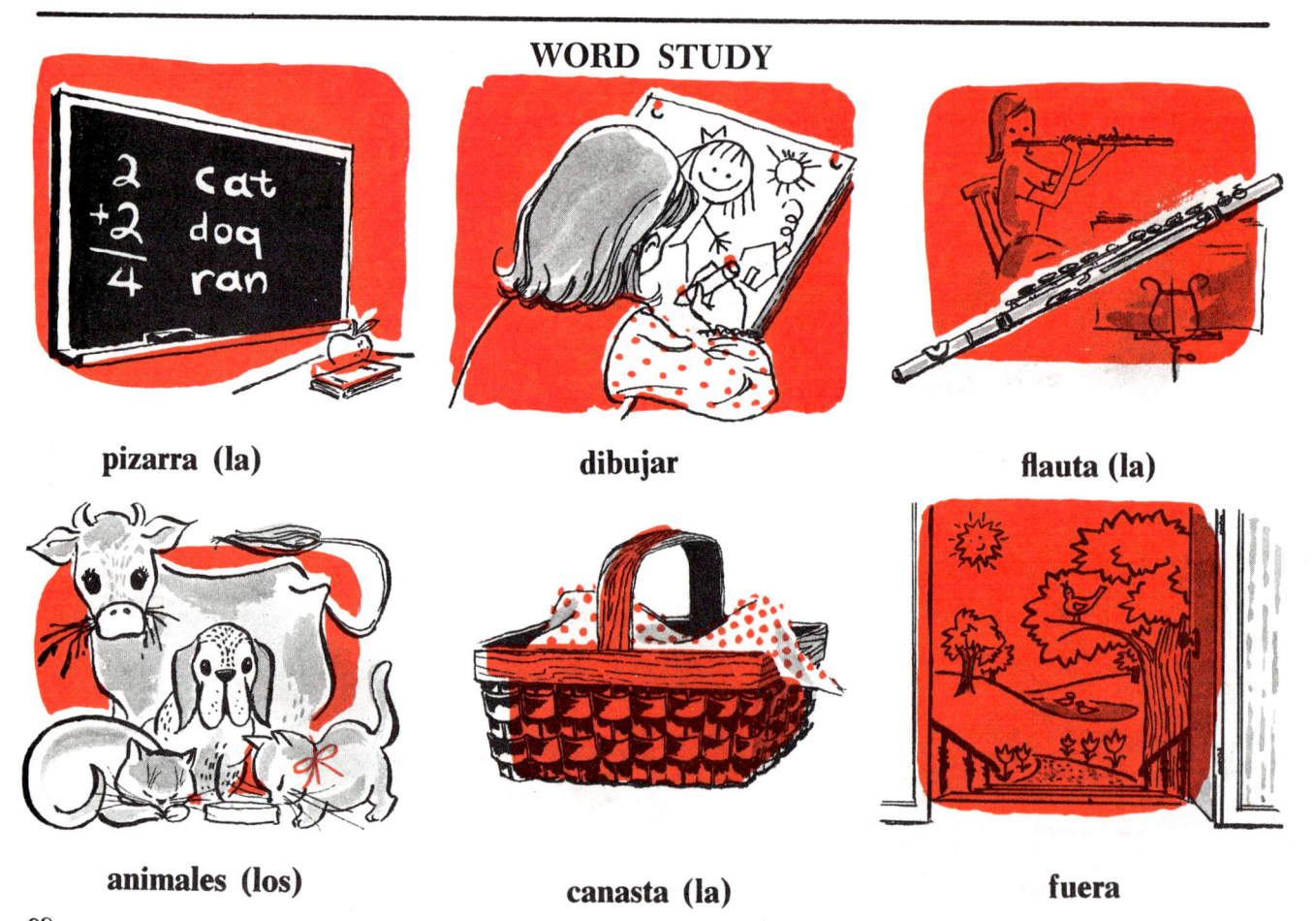

WORD STUDY

pizarra (la)

dibujar

flauta (la)

animales (los)

canasta (la)

fuera

LECCIÓN 27

¿QUIERES VENIR A UNA FIESTA?

Robert is going to celebrate his birthday soon. Helen thinks she needs new clothes for the party. And—surprise, surprise—her mother agrees with her.

Elena—Mamá, mamá. Roberto va a cumplir diez años. Su mamá va a dar una fiesta para él. ¿Puedo ir, mamá?—La mamá de Roberto va a telefonear.

Mamá—Muy bien.

Elena—Mamá, el teléfono.

Mamá—Sí, habla la señora Sánchez. Ah, señora Pérez. ¿Cómo está?... Muy bien, gracias. ¿Cuándo? ¿El día veinte y ocho? ¿A qué hora? A las cuatro?
   Muchas gracias. Adiós.

Elena—Mamá, ¿qué me pongo? Necesito un traje nuevo.

Mamá—Tienes razón. Vamos a las tiendas mañana. También vamos a comprar un regalo para Roberto.

Elena—Mamá. También necesito zapatos.

Vendedora—¿Qué desea usted, señora?

Mamá—Deseo ver unos trajes de nilón.

Vendedora—Aquí hay un traje muy bonito.

Elena—No, mamá, no me gusta. Quiero una falda plegada.

Vendedora—Aquí hay un traje azul con falda plegada. ¿Quieres probarte éste?

Elena—Sí. Me gusta mucho.

Mamá—¿Cuánto cuesta?

Vendedora—Sólo doce dólares.

Elena—Mamá, di que sí.

Vendedora—¿Desea algo más?

Mamá—Sí. Un par de zapatos?

Vendedora—Por aquí, por favor. ¿De qué color desea usted los zapatos?

Mamá—Blancos, de cuero.

Vendedora—¿Desea algo más, señora?

Mamá—Nada más, señorita, gracias.

Vendedora—Muchas gracias. Hasta la vista.

LESSON 27

DO YOU WANT TO COME TO A PARTY?

Helen—Mother, Mother. Robert's going to be ten years old. His mother is going to have a birthday party for him. May I go, Mother? Robert's mother is going to phone you.

Mother—Very well.

Helen—Mother, the telephone.

Mother—Yes. It is Mrs. Sanchez speaking. Ah, Mrs. Perez. How are you?—Very well, thank you. When? On the 28th? At what time? At four o'clock? Thank you very much. Good-by.

Helen—Mother. What shall I wear? I need a new dress.

Mother—You're right. We'll go shopping tomorrow. We'll also buy a gift for Robert.

Helen—Mother, I need shoes, too.

Saleswoman—What do you wish, madam?

Mother—I want to see some nylon dresses.

Saleswoman—Here's a very pretty dress.

Helen—No, mama, I don't like it. I want a pleated skirt.

Saleswoman—Here's a blue dress with a pleated skirt. Do you want to try it on?

Helen—Yes, I like it very much.

Mother—How much does it cost?

Saleswoman—Only twelve dollars.

Helen—Mother, say yes.

Saleswoman—Do you wish something else?

Mother—Yes, a pair of shoes.

Saleswoman—Through here, please. What color shoes do you wish?

Mother—White leather.

Saleswoman—Do you wish something else, madam?

Mother—Nothing more. Thank you, Miss.

Saleswoman—Thank you very much. Call again.

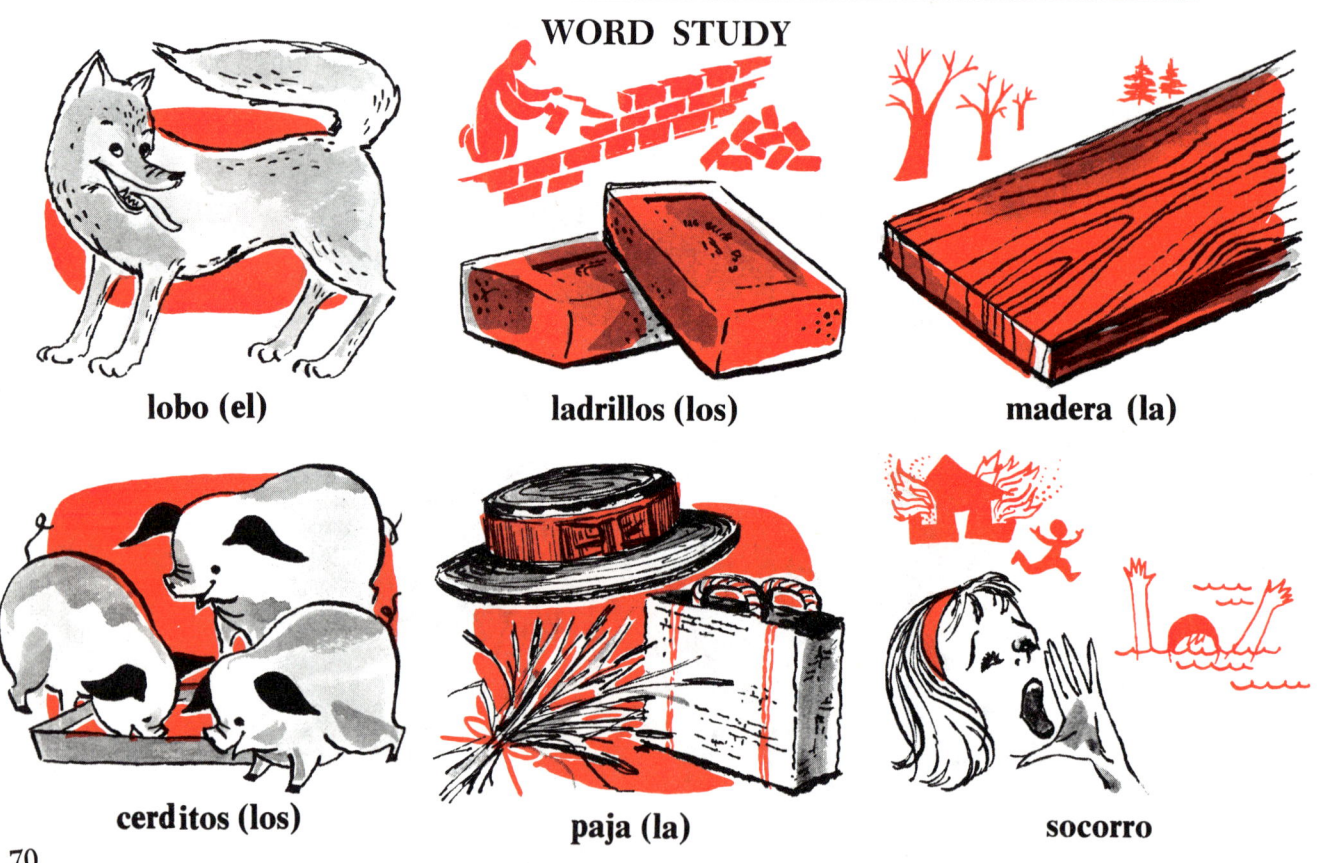

WORD STUDY

lobo (el)

ladrillos (los)

madera (la)

cerditos (los)

paja (la)

socorro

LECCIÓN 28

LA FIESTA DE CUMPLEAÑOS

Some birthday customs are different in other lands, as you will learn later. Some are the same. Listen carefully to find out which customs at Robert's party are familiar to you.

Roberto—Bienvenida, Elena.

Elena—Feliz cumpleaños, Roberto. Este regalo es para tí.

Roberto—Muchas gracias, Elena.

La mamá de R.—Bienvenida, Elena. ¡Qué traje tan lindo! Me gusta mucho la falda plegada.

Elena—Gracias, señora.

Juana—Buenas tardes, Elena. ¡Qué traje tan bonito!

Elena—Muchas gracias, Juana. Tu traje es muy bonito también.

La mamá de R.—Vamos a tomar refrescos ahora. Roberto va a partir el bizcocho.

Elena—¡Qué mesa tan linda!

La mamá de R.—¿Quién quiere helado de vainilla?

Juana, Susana, etc.—¡Yo, yo, yo!

La mamá de R.—Y ahora, Roberto, el bizcocho.

Juana—¡Qué bizcocho tan lindo! ¿Cuántas velitas tiene?

Susana—Tiene once velitas.

La mamá de R.—Vamos a cantar todos:

> Cumpleaños feliz,
> Cumpleaños feliz,
> Felicidades Roberto,
> Felicidades a tí.

Todos—Sopla, Roberto, sopla.

La mamá de R.—Vamos a jugar a las sillas musicales. Yo voy a tocar el piano. No olviden, cuando para la música, tienen que buscar una silla vacía.

Roberto—Mamá, ¿podemos romper la piñata ahora?

La mamá de R.—Ahora no. Espera un poco. Tu papá va a colgarla. Ahora podemos ver la película.

Todos—¡Qué bueno! ¡Magnífico! ¿Cómo se llama la película?

Roberto—Se llama "En El Jardín Zoológico."

LESSON 28

THE BIRTHDAY PARTY

Robert—Welcome, Helen.

Helen—Happy birthday, Robert. Here is a present for you.

Robert—Many thanks, Helen.

Robert's mother—Welcome, Helen. What a pretty dress! I like the pleated skirt.

Helen—Thank you, ma'am.

Joan—Good afternoon Helen. What a pretty dress!

Helen—Many thanks, Joan. Your dress is very pretty too.

Robert's mother—Let's have some refreshments now. Robert is going to cut the cake.

Helen—What a pretty table!

Robert's mother—Who wants vanilla ice cream?

Joan, Susan, etc.—Me, me, me.

Robert's mother—Who wants chocolate ice cream?

Joan, Helen, etc.—Me, me, me.

Robert's mother—And now, Robert, the cake.

Joan—What a pretty cake. How many candles does it have?

Susan—It has eleven candles.

Robert's mother—Let's all sing.

> Happy birthday
> Happy birthday
> Congratulations, Robert
> Congratulations to you.

All—Blow, Robert, blow.

Robert's mother—Let's play musical chairs. I am going to play the piano. Don't forget. When the music stops you have to look for an empty chair.

Robert—Mother, may we break the "piñata" now?

Robert's mother—Not now, wait a little. Papa is going to hang it up. Now we can see the film.

All—How nice! Wonderful! What's the name of the film?

Robert—It's called, "At The Zoo."

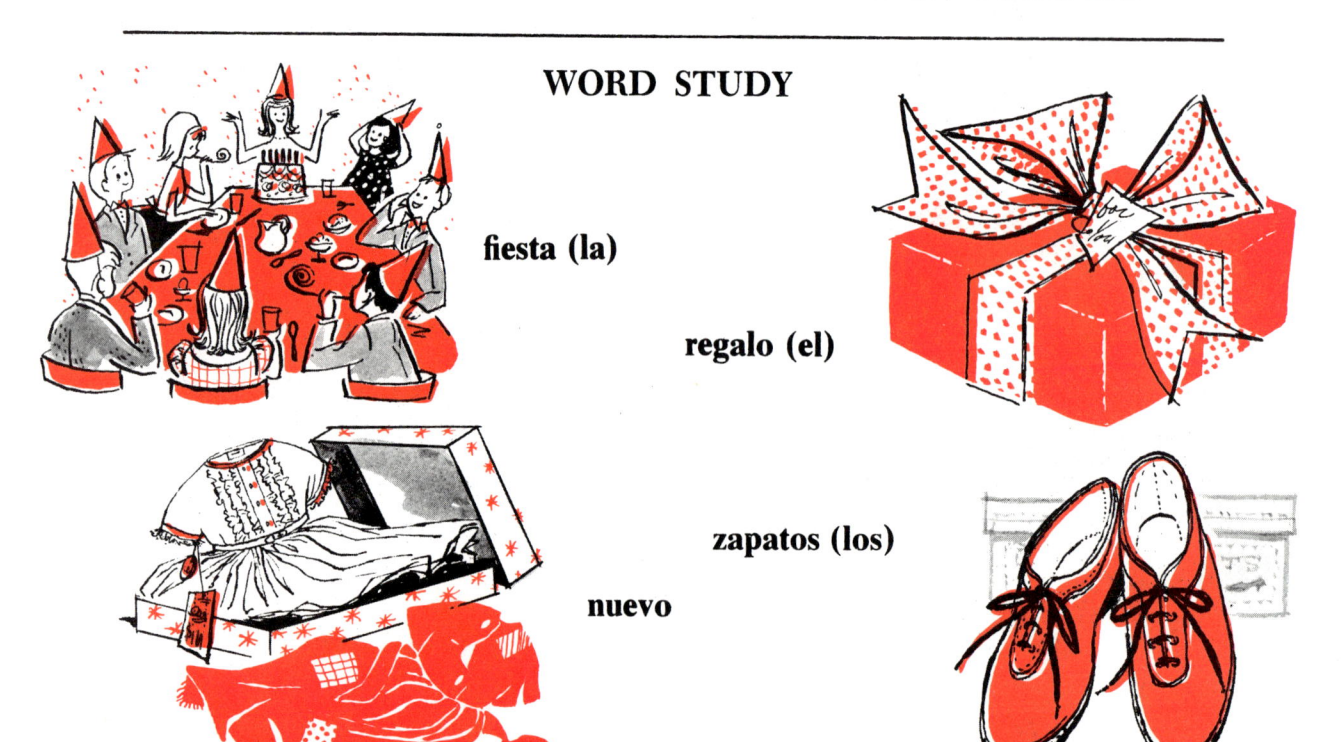

WORD STUDY

fiesta (la)

regalo (el)

nuevo

zapatos (los)

LECCIÓN 29

¿QUIÉN PUEDE ROMPER LA PIÑATA?

The practice of breaking a gift-filled earthenware pot at a party is new to many of us. Why don't you find out how it's done? You may want to try it yourself sometime.

Roberto—Vamos a romper la piñata. ¿Quién quiere ser el primero?
Todos—¡Yo, yo!
Roberto—Entonces, primero las niñas. ¿Juana? Cada uno tiene tres turnos.
Todos—¡Más arriba . . . más abajo . . . al centro . . . ! ¡Rómpela! No, Juana. Le toca a Rosa ahora.
Todos—¡Más abajo . . . al centro . . . no . . . más arriba!
Roberto—No, Rosa. Ahora les toca a los niños. ¿Pedro?
Todos—¡Más abajo . . . más fuerte . . . más arriba! ¡Caramba!
Roberto—Esta piñata no se rompe. Voy a probar yo.
Todos—¡Más fuerte . . . al centro . . . más arriba! ¡Eso es! ¡Olé, Roberto!
La mamá de R.—Roberto, ¿quieres abrir tus regalos ahora?
Todos—Sí, sí, Roberto. Abre tus regalos. Queremos ver tus regalos.
Roberto—Gracias, Juana. Estos guantes son muy lindos.
Juana—De nada, Roberto.
Roberto—Gracias, Elena. Este libro de sellos es un regalo precioso.
Elena—De nada, Roberto.
Roberto—¡Muy, Pedro! Esta pelota de béisbol me encanta. Gracias.
Pedro—De nada, Roberto.
Roberto—Muchas gracias a todos.
Todos—Muchas gracias a tí Roberto. Muchas gracias a usted, señora. Nos divertimos mucho.
Pedro—En México y en otros países latinoamericanos, la canción de cumpleaños es:

Las Mañanitas

Estas son las mañanitas que cantaba el Rey David
A las muchachas bonitas, se las cantaban así:
Despierta, mi bien, despierta, mira que ya amaneció,
Ya los pajarillos cantan. La luna ya se metió.

LESSON 29

WHO CAN BREAK THE PIÑATA?

Robert—We are going to break the "piñata." Who wants to be the first?
All the children—Me, me.
Robert—Well then, the girls first. Joan? Each one has three tries.
All the children—Higher; lower; to the center. Break it. No, Joan. Give it to Rose now.
All the children—Lower; to the center; no; higher.
Robert—No, Rose. Give it to the boys now. Peter?
All the children—Lower; stronger; higher; caramba.
Robert—This piñata is not breaking. I'm going to try.
All the children—Harder; to the center; higher; that's it. Olé, Robert.
Robert's mother—Robert, do you want to open your presents now?
All the children—Yes, yes, Robert. Open your presents. We want to see your presents.
Robert—Thank you, Joan. These gloves are very pretty.
Joan—You're welcome, Robert.
Robert—Thank you, Helen. This stamp book is a beautiful present.
Helen—You're welcome, Robert.
Robert—Wow, Peter, this baseball thrills me. Thanks.
Peter—You're welcome, Robert.
Robert—Thank you very much, everyone.
All the children—Thank you very much, Robert. Thank you very much, ma'am. We had a very good time.
Peter—In Mexico and in other Latin American countries the birthday song is:

Daybreak

These are the daybreak songs that King David sang
To the pretty girls, they were sung thus:
Wake, my love, awaken. See that it is already dawn
The little birds are singing already and the moon has disappeared.

WORD STUDY

helado (el)   **colgar**   **velita (la)**

LECCIÓN 30

¡AY, AY, TENGO DOLOR DE ESTÓMAGO!

Oh! Oh! Too much birthday party brings the expected "tummy" ache.

Mamá—Elena, son las nueve. Levántate, por favor.
Elena—Mamá, no puedo levantarme. Estoy enferma.
Mamá—¿Estás enferma? ¿Qué tienes?
Elena—Tengo dolor de estómago. ¡Ay, tengo dolor de cabeza!
Mamá—¿Qué puede ser? ¡Ah, sí, la fiesta de Roberto! Demasiados dulces, helados y bizcocho.
Elena—No, mamá. Me comí sólo tres helados.
Mamá—¿Tres helados? ¿Y cuántos pedazos de bizcocho?
Elena—Sólo dos, mamá. ¡Ay, tengo dolor de muelas también!
Mamá—Tienes fiebre. Voy a llamar al doctor.
Mamá—¿Doctor Pagán? Habla la señora Sánchez. Elena está enferma. Tiene dolor de estómago y de cabeza. Tiene dolor de muelas. Tiene fiebre.
  Muchas gracias, doctor.
Elena—¡Ay, mamá! Tengo dolores.
Mamá—Yo sé, nena. Tómate esta medicina.
Elena—¡No quiero tomar la medicina! ¡Ay!
Mamá—Vamos, nena, tómate esta cucharadita de medicina.
Elena—Mamá, ¿puedes leerme un cuento?
Mamá—Sí, Elena, ¿cómo no? ¿Cuál cuento quieres oír?
Elena—Mamá, no sé. Léeme un cuento bueno.
Mamá—Sí, nena. Voy a buscar el libro.

Vamos a cantar:

Hoy es lunes, hoy es lunes,
¿Qué comer? ¿Qué comer?
Lunes las legumbres, lunes las legumbres,
Mmmm.
Hoy es martes, hoy es martes,
¿Qué comer? ¿Qué comer?
Martes las naranjas, martes las naranjas,
Mmmm.
Es domingo, es domingo,
Algo hay de todo, algo hay de todo,
Y de este modo,
¡Ay de mí, ay de mí!

LESSON 30

OH! OH! I HAVE A STOMACH ACHE

Mother—Helen, it's nine o'clock. Get up, please.
Helen—Mama, I can't get up. I'm sick.
Mother—You're sick? What's the matter with you?
Helen—I have a stomach-ache. Ouch, I have a headache.
Mother—What can it be? Ah, yes, Robert's party. Too many candies, ice cream and cake, I believe.
Helen—No, Mother, I only ate three ice creams.
Mother—Three ice creams? And how many pieces of cake?
Helen—Only two, Mama. Ouch, I have a toothache, too.
Mother—You have fever. I'm going to call the doctor.
Mother—Doctor Pagán, Mrs. Sanchez speaking. Helen is ill. She has a stomach-ache and a headache. She has a toothache. She has fever. Thank you, doctor.
Helen—Ouch, Mother. I have a pain.
Mother—I know, child. Take this medicine.
Helen—I don't want to take the medicine. Ouch!
Mother—Come, child, take this teaspoonful of medicine.

Helen—Mother, can you read me a story?
Mother—Yes, Helen, of course. Which story do you want to hear.
Helen—Mother, I don't know. Read me a good story.
Mother—Yes, child. I'll go get the book.

Let's Sing!

It is Monday, it is Monday
What to eat? What to eat?
Monday, the vegetables
Monday, the vegetables
Mmmm.
It is Tuesday. It is Tuesday.
What to eat? What to eat?
Tuesday the orange,
Tuesday the orange,
Mmmm.
It is Sunday. It is Sunday.
There is something of everything,
There is something of everything,
And in this way,
Poor me! Poor me!
Mmmm.

WORD STUDY

pelota (la)

Estoy enfermo(a).

película (la)

LECCIÓN 31

CAPERUCITA ROJA

Helen's tummy ache brings to mind a well known story in which a wolf pretends to be ill. Do you know which story we mean? Listen to find out if you're right.

Este es el cuento que lee la mamá de Elena.

Había una vez una niña muy linda. La niña se llama Caperucita Roja. Caperucita Roja vive con su madre en una casa cerca de un bosque. Un día la mamá de Caperucita Roja la llama:

—Caperucita Roja.

—Sí, mamá. Aquí estoy. ¿Qué deseas?

—Caperucita Roja: la abuelita está enferma. Tiene dolor de cabeza y dolor de garganta. Hazme el favor de ir a su casa y de llevarle esta canasta de frutas.

—Con mucho gusto, mamacita.

La mamá le da la canasta de frutas a Caperucita Roja. Le dice:—Hasta luego, Caperucita. Dame un beso. Ten cuidado con el bosque. No te pares.

—Adiós, mamacita. No te apures. Regreso en seguida.

Y Caperucita Roja empieza a caminar por el bosque. Después de unos minutos, aparece un lobo.

—Buenos días, niña,—le dice el mal lobo.— ¿Cómo te llamas?

—Me llamo Caperucita Roja. Y ¿cómo se llama usted, señor?

—Me llamo el señor Lobo.

—Mucho gusto, señor Lobo.

—Mucho gusto, Caperucita Roja. ¿Adónde vas, Caperucita Roja?

—Voy a casa de mi abuelita. Mi pobre **abuelita** está enferma.

—Tú eres una niña buena. Caperucita **Roja**. Y . . . ¿dónde vive tu abuelita?

—Vive en la casa blanca en el bosque.

—Yo tengo que ir cerca de la casa de tu abuelita. Vamos a ver quién llega primero a la **casa** de tu abuelita.

—Muy bien, señor Lobo. Hasta luego.

El mal lobo corre y corre y pronto llega a la casa de la abuelita.

—¡Tan!¡Tan!

Elena—Mamá, alguien llama a la puerta.
Mamá—Voy a ver . . . Pasen, pasen. Elena, son tus amigos.
Elena—Estoy enferma. Mamá está leyendo el cuento de Caperucita Roja. ¿Mamá, pueden quedarse mis amigos?
Mamá—Con mucho gusto.

77

LESSON 31

LITTLE RED RIDING HOOD

This is the story that Helen's mother reads:

Once upon a time there was a very pretty little girl. She is called Little Red Riding Hood. Little Red Riding Hood lives with her mother in a house near the forest. One day, Little Red Riding Hood's mother calls her: "Little Red Riding Hood."

"Yes, Mother. Here I am. What do you wish?"

"Red Riding Hood, Grandmama is ill. She has a headache and a sore throat. Please, do me the favor of going to her house and of taking her this basket of fruits."

"Gladly, Mother dear."

The mother gives the basket of fruits to Little Red Riding Hood. She says, "See you later, Red Riding Hood. Give me a kiss. Be careful in the forest. Don't stop."

"Good-by, mother dear. Don't worry. I'll return promptly."

And Little Red Riding Hood begins walking through the forest. After a few minutes a wolf appears.

"Good day, child," says the bad wolf. "What's your name?"

"My name is Little Red Riding Hood. And what is your name, sir?"

"My name is Mr. Wolf."

"Pleased to meet you, Mr. Wolf."

"Pleased to meet you, Little Red Riding Hood. Where are you going, Little Red Riding Hood?"

"I'm going to my grandmama's house. My poor grandmama is ill."

"You're a good girl, Little Red Riding Hood. And . . . where does your grandmama live?"

"She lives in the white house, in the forest."

"I must go near your grandmama's house. Let's see who gets to your grandmama's house first."

"Very well, Mr. Wolf. See you later."

The bad wolf runs and runs and arrives quickly at the home of the grandmother.

(knock, knock)

Helen—Mother! I think someone is knocking at the door.
Mother—I'm going to see. Come in, come in. . . . Helen, it's your friends.
Helen—I'm sick. But Mother is reading the story of Little Red Riding Hood. Mother, may my friends stay?
Mother—Gladly.

QUIZ 9

Let's play a game of *Sí* or *No*, shall we?
1. Roberto va a cumplir quince años.
2. Elena necesita un sobretodo nuevo.
3. Roberto va a partir el bizcocho.
4. Pedro rompe la piñata.

Turn to page 80 to see if you have answered correctly.

LECCIÓN 32

¿QUIÉN TIENE MIEDO? ¿YO? ¡OH, NO!

What do you think Red Riding Hood does after the woodcutter rescues her?

Elena—Continúa, mamá.
Mamá—(¡Tan! ¡Tan!)
 —¿Quién es?
 —Soy yo, Caperucita Roja.

 —Muy bien, entra. La puerta está abierta.
 El mal lobo entra y salta a la cama para comerse a la abuelita. Pero la abuelita salta de la cama y se esconde en el armario. Pronto, el lobo se pone la ropa de la abuela y espera a Caperucita Roja en la cama de la abuela.
 Por fin, Caperucita Roja llega a la casa de la abuelita y llama a la puerta.
 ¡Tan! ¡Tan!
 —¿Quién es?—, dice el mal lobo imitando la voz de la abuelita.
 —Soy yo, Caperucita Roja.
 —Muy bien. Entra, Caperucita Roja. La puerta está abierta.

Caperucita Roja entra en el cuarto y dice:
—Buenos días, abuelita. ¿Cómo estás?
 —Buenos días, Caperucita Roja. Estoy muy enferma.
 Caperucita Roja mira a su abuela.
 —Abuelita, ¿por qué tienes las orejas tan grandes?
 —Para oírte mejor, nena.
 —Abuelita, ¿por qué tienes los ojos tan grandes?
 —Para verte mejor, nena.
 —Abuelita, ¿por qué tienes los brazos tan largos?
 —Para abrazarte mejor, Caperucita.
 —Pero, abuelita, ¿por qué tienes la boca tan grande?
 —Para comerme a Caperucita Roja.
 El lobo salta de la cama para comerse a Caperucita Roja. Un leñador que está trabajando muy cerca, oye los gritos de Caperucita Roja y corre a la casa, y mata al lobo.

La abuela sale del armario y le da las gracias al leñador. Caperucita Roja también le da las gracias al leñador.

LESSON 32

WHO'S AFRAID? NOT ME!

Helen—Continue, Mother.
Mother—(knock, knock) "Who is it?"
"It's I, Little Red Riding Hood."
"Very well, enter. The door is open."
The bad wolf enters and jumps on the bed to eat up the grandmother. But the grandmother jumps from the bed and hides herself in the closet. Quickly, the bad wolf puts on the grandmother's clothes. He waits for Little Red Riding Hood in the grandmother's bed.
Finally Little Red Riding Hood reaches the grandmother's house and knocks on the door.
(knock, knock)
"Who is it?" says the bad wolf, imitating the grandmother's voice.
"It is I, Little Red Riding Hood."
"Very well. Enter, Little Red Riding Hood. The door is open."
Little Red Riding Hood enters the room and says, "Good morning, Grandmama. How are you?"
"Good morning, Little Red Riding Hood. I'm very ill."
Little Red Riding Hood looks at her grandmother.
"Grandmama, why do you have such large ears?"
"To hear you better, child."
"Grandmama, why do you have such large eyes?"
"To see you better, child."
"Grandmama, why do you have such long arms?"
"To embrace you better, child."
"But, Grandmama, why do you have such a large mouth?"
"To eat Little Red Riding Hood!"
The wolf jumps from the bed to eat up Little Red Riding Hood.
A woodcutter who is working very close by hears Little Red Riding Hood's screams and runs to the house. He kills the wolf.
The grandmother comes out of the closet and thanks the woodcutter. Little Red Riding Hood thanks the woodcutter, too.

ANSWERS TO QUIZ 9

1. *No.* Roberto va a cumplir diez años.
2. *No.* Elena necesita un sobretodo nuevo.
3. *Sí.* Roberto va a partir el bizcocho.
4. *No.* Roberto rompe la piñata.

LECCIÓN 33

VIENE EL CIRCO

Everyone loves the circus. Helen and Robert do, too. Is there any act you'd rather not look at? I wonder if it's the same one that Helen doesn't want to watch?

Elena—Papá, papá, viene el circo.
Papá—¿Cuándo?
Elena—El cuatro de abril. ¿Podemos ir al circo?

Papá—Vamos a ver.

Mamá—¿Por qué lloras, Elena?
Elena—Papá no quiere ir al circo. Yo quiero ir al circo. Todos mis amigos tienen ya los billetes.
Mamá—No te apures.
Elena—Gracias, mamá.
Mamá—¡Bueno! Elena, papá va a comprar los billetes hoy mismo.

Elena—Papá, dame dinero por favor para maní.
Papá—Aquí tienes dinero. Compra un paquete de maní para Roberto también.
Elena—Gracias, papá.

Todos—¡Qué asientos tan buenos! Se ve todo. Estamos en el centro.
Roberto—¡Ya empieza, ya empieza! ¡Qué música tan bonita!
Elena—¡Qué desfile tan bonito! ¡Mira los leones y los elefantes!

Elena—¡Cómo saltan los payasos! ¡Qué trajes tan lindos llevan las bailarinas!
Anunciador—Señoras y señores. Atención. Van a ver un número espectacular. Vamos a meter a este hombre en cañón y vamos a dispararlo.
Elena—Tengo miedo. No quiero mirar.
Roberto—¡Qué tonta! No es nada.
Elena—Yo prefiero ver el acto de los perritos. Son tan lindos.
El papá de Elena—Un espectáculo maravilloso, ¿verdad?
El papá de Roberto—Sí, magnífico.

Vamos a cantar:

Uno de enero, dos de febrero,
Tres de marzo, cuatro de abril,
Cinco de mayo, seis de junio,
Siete de julio, San Fermín,
Tra, la, la, la, la, la, la
¿Quién ha roto la pandereta?
Tra, la, la, la, la, la, la
El que la ha roto, la pagará.

LESSON 33

THE CIRCUS IS COMING

Helen—Father, Father! The circus is coming!
Father—When?
Helen—The fourth of April. Can we go to the circus?
Father—We'll see.

Mother—Why are you crying, Helen?
Helen—Papa doesn't want to go to the circus. I want to go to the circus. All my friends have the tickets already.
Mother—Don't worry.
Helen—Thank you, Mother.
Mother—Fine, Helen. Father will go to buy the tickets this very day.

Helen—Papa, give me money, please, for peanuts.
Father—Here is money. Buy a bag of peanuts for Robert, too.
Helen—Thank you, Father.

All—What wonderful seats. You can see everything. We're in the center.
Robert—It's beginning, it's beginning. What pretty music!
Helen—What a wonderful parade! Look at the lions and the elephants. How the clowns jump! What wonderful dresses the dancers are wearing!
Master of Ceremonies—Ladies and Gentlemen. Your attention. You're going to see a spectacular number. We're going to place this man in a cannon and we're going to shoot him out.
Helen—I'm afraid. I don't want to look.
Robert—What a silly girl. It's nothing.
Helen—I prefer to see the little dog act. They're so pretty.

Helen's Father—A marvelous spectacle. Don't you think so?
Robert's Father—Yes, wonderful.

Let's Sing!
The first of January, second of February,
Third of March, Fourth of April,
Fifth of May, sixth of June,
Seventh of July, Saint Fermín
Tra, la, la, la, la, la, la
Who has broken the tambourine?
Tra, la, la, la, la, la, la
The one who has broken it will pay for it.

WORD STUDY

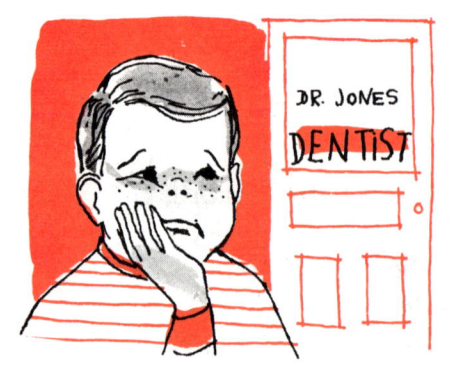

dolor de muelas (el) 　　　**estómago (el)** 　　　**lunes (el)**

LECCIÓN 34

UN PICNIC

Spring brings thoughts of picnics and outdoor fun, doesn't it? Listen to how easy it is to talk about a picnic in Spanish. So many of the words are the same in both languages.

Mamá—Por fin, hace buen tiempo. La primavera es mi estación favorita. En el invierno hace demasiado frío; en el verano hace demasiado calor.

Elena—¿No te gusta el otoño? En el otoño no hace demasiado frío y no hace demasiado calor.

Mamá—Sí, me gusta el otoño pero prefiero la primavera.

Elena—Mamá. ¿Podemos ir de picnic este domingo?

Mamá—¿Por qué no? ¿Quieres invitar a tus amigos?

Elena—Mamá, tú eres un verdadero amor. ¿A qué hora salimos?

Mamá—A las diez.

Elena—Mamá, por favor: ¿puedes llamar a los padres de cada uno por teléfono?

Mamá—Sí. ¡Cómo no!

Mamá—Éste es un sitio muy lindo, ¿verdad?

Elena—Sí, mamá, el lago está muy cerca y mira, el horno para cocinar los "hamburgers" y los perros calientes.

Mamá—Magnífico. Toma otro "sandwich," Roberto. Elena, come las papas fritas. Juana, ¿otro vaso de leche? Juan, ¿otro "hamburger"?

Juan—No, gracias, señora, no puedo comer más.

Elena—Vamos a jugar al escondite.

Mamá—Sí, pero por aquí cerca.

Elena—No te apures, mamá.

Mamá—Carlos, por favor, ve a llamar a los niños. Son las cuatro.

Papá—Niños. Tenemos que regresar a casa.

Elena—¡Oh, todavía no, papá!

Todos—¡Oh, no, señor! Es demasiado temprano.

Papá—Ya es hora. Pero podemos volver la semana que viene si sus padres lo permiten.

Todos—Gracias, gracias. ¡Qué bueno!

LESSON 34

A PICNIC

Mother—Finally, the weather is fine. Spring is my favorite season. In winter, it's too cold; in summer it's too hot.
Helen—Don't you like autumn? It's not too cold and it's not too hot in autumn.
Mother—Yes. I like autumn, but I prefer spring.
Helen—Mother. Can we go on a picnic this Sunday?
Mother—Why not? Do you want to invite your friends?
Helen—Mother, you're a real love. At what time are we going out?
Mother—At ten o'clock.
Helen—Mother, please can you call the parents of each one by telephone?
Mother—Yes, of course.

Mother—This is a very pretty site, isn't it?
Helen—Yes, Mother, the lake is very close by, and look, the oven for cooking the hamburgers and the hot dogs.
Mother—Wonderful. Take another sandwich, Robert. Helen, eat the fried potatoes. Joan, another glass of milk? John, another hamburger?
Joan—No, thank you, ma'am. I can't take more.

Helen—Let's play "Hide and Seek."
Mother—Yes, but near here.
Helen—Don't worry, Mother.

Mother—Charles, go call the children, please. It's four o'clock.
Father—Children, we have to go back home.
Helen—Oh, not yet, father.
The other children—Oh, no, sir. It's too early.
Father—It's time. But we can come next week if your parents permit.
All the children—Thank you, thank you. How wonderful!

WORD STUDY

legumbres (las)   **domingo (el)**   **abuelita (la)**

LECCIÓN 35

A LA PLAYA

What does summertime make you think of? Would you like to join our friends at the beach right now?

Papá—¡Qué calor!
Mamá—Sí, hace mucho calor. Estamos en julio.
Papá—¿Por qué no damos un paseo en auto y vamos a la playa?
Papá—¿Dónde están los trajes de baño?

Mamá—Los trajes de baño están en mi armario.
Papá—¿Dónde están las zapatillas?
Mamá—Están en el armario también.
Elena—Mamá, ¿dónde está la pelota grande?
Mamá—Está en el cuarto de Carlitos.
Elena—¿Dónde están las palas?
Mamá—Tenemos que comprar palas nuevas.
Elena—Entonces yo quiero una pala roja.
Mamá—Bueno. Vamos ya.
Elena—Mamá, ¿puedo invitar a Roberto?
Mamá—Sí. Con mucho gusto.
Elena—Gracias, mamá. Voy a telefonear a Roberto.

Papá—Este sitio es bueno. No hay mucha gente.
Elena—Sí. Y se ve el mar.
Mamá—Y no hay mucho sol. ¿Te gusta este sitio, Elena? ¿Te gusta este sitio, Elena? ¿Te gusta, Roberto?
Elena y Roberto—Sí, mucho, mucho.
Elena—Papá, ¿puedo cubrirte con arena con mi pala nueva?

Papá—Sí, Elena . . . ¡Oh, no, Carlitos, no los ojos en, en la cabeza no!
Mamá—Niños, ¿quieren entrar al agua conmigo? Vamos a nadar.
Elena y Roberto—Con mucho gusto.
Mamá—Carlos, regresamos en seguida.
Papá—¿A qué hora vamos a comer?
Elena—Sí, mamá, ¿a qué hora vamos a comer?
Mamá—¡Ja, ja! ¡Qué familia tengo yo! Vamos, Elena, el agua va a darte aún más apetito.
Elena—Mamá, eso no es posible. Siempre tengo hambre.
Mamá—Bueno. Vamos a nadar. Regresamos en seguida. Papá va a sacar de la canasta los platos, los tenedores y los vasos de papel.
Elena—Papacito: no olvides de sacar la comida también.

LESSON 35

AT THE BEACH

Father—What heat!
Mother—Yes, it's hot. It is the month of July.
Father—Why don't we take a ride in the auto and go to the beach.
Father—Where are the bathing suits?
Mother—The bathing suits are in my closet.
Father—Where are the bathing slippers?
Mother—They're in the closet, too.
Helen—Mama, where is the large ball?
Mother—It's in little Charles' room.
Helen—Where are the shovels?
Mother—I believe we have to buy new shovels.
Helen—Then I want a red shovel.
Mother—All right. Let's go now.
Helen—Mother. May I invite Robert?
Mother—Yes. Gladly.
Helen—Thank you, Mother. I'm going to telephone Robert.

Father—This spot is good. There aren't many people.
Helen—Yes. And you can see the sea.
Mother—And there isn't much sun. Do you like this spot, Helen? Do you like it, Robert?
Helen and Robert—Yes, a lot, a lot.
Helen—Father, may I cover you with sand with my new shovel?
Father—Yes, Helen. Oh, no, Charlie! Not in the eyes and not on the head!
Mother—Children do you want to go into the water with me? Let's go swimming.
Helen—Gladly. I know how to swim well now.
Mother—Charles, we'll be back soon.
Father—What time are we going to eat?
Helen—Yes, Mama. What time are we going to eat?
Mother—Ha, ha. What a family I have. Let's go, Helen, the water will give you even more appetite.
Helen—Mama, that's not possible. I'm always hungry.
Mother—Good. Let's go swimming. We'll be right back. Father will take the paper plates, forks and glasses from the basket.
Helen—Father dear. Don't forget to take out the food too.

WORD STUDY

Caperucita Roja   **cama (la)**   **puerta (la)**

LECCIÓN 36

UNA CARTA DE LOS ABUELOS

Are you fortunate enough to have your grandparents living close by? If you're not, I guess a letter from them is fun, too.

Mamá—Elena. Alguien llama a la puerta. ¿Quién es?

Elena—Es el cartero.

Mamá—¿Hay cartas para mí?

Elena—Sí. Hay una. Mamá, es de los abuelitos.

Mamá—La abuela escribe:

Querida Clara:

¿Por qué no vienen a pasar el fin de semana en la finca? Pueden venir el viernes por la tarde. El campo está muy lindo en este mes de noviembre. Hace un tiempo magnífico.

Llámame por teléfono y dime cuándo vienen.

Todo el cariño de
Mamá.

Elena—Mamá, vamos a la finca.

Mamá—No sé. Tengo que hablar con tu papá.

Elena—Llama a papá por teléfono ahora mismo, mamá.

Mamá—Bueno.

Mamá—Carlos, habla Clara. Tengo una carta de mamá. Dice que el campo está muy lindo.

—¿Qué dices? ¿Qué tiempo hace?

Mamá dice que hace un tiempo magnífico. ¿Este fin de semana? Muy bien. Gracias.

Mamá—Elena, vamos a la finca este fin de semana.

Elena—Magnífico. Se lo voy a decir a mis amigos.

Mamá—Espera, espera. La carta de la abuela me recuerda que tú no sabes escribir los meses del año. Y tus abuelos van a hacerte muchas preguntas. Mira, escucha y repite después de mí:

enero, febrero, marzo, abril, mayo, junio, julio, agosto, septiembre, octubre, noviembre y diciembre.

Y ahora escribe los meses aquí.

Hay un poema para recordar los meses y los días de cada mes.

Elena—¿Cómo es, mamá?

Mamá—Trienta días trae septiembre con abril, junio y noviembre Veinte y ocho tiene uno y los demás treinta y uno.

LESSON 36

A LETTER FROM GRANDMOTHER AND GRANDFATHER

Mother—Helen, someone is knocking at the door. Who is it?
Helen—It's the mailman.
Mother—Are there letters for me?
Helen—Yes, here's one. Mother, it's from Grandfather and Grandmother.
Mother—Grandmother writes:

Dear Clara,
Why don't you come to spend the week-end at the farm? You can come Friday afternoon. The country is very pretty [this] month of November. The weather is magnificent.
Call me by telephone and tell me when you're coming.

All the affection of
Mother

Helen—Mother, let's go to the farm.
Mother—I don't know. I have to talk to Father.
Helen—Call Father by telephone right now, Mother.
Mother—Good.
Mother—Charles? Clara talking. I have a letter from Mother. They want to see us. She says the country is very pretty. What do you say? How is the weather? Mother says the weather is wonderful. This week-end? Fine. Thanks. I'm going to call Mother immediately.
Mother—Helen, we're going to the farm this week-end.
Helen—Wonderful! I'm going to tell my friends.
Mother—Wait, wait. In her letter Grandmother reminds me that you don't know how to write the months of the year. And your grandparents will ask many questions. Look, listen and repeat after me:

January, February, March, April,
May, June, July, August, September,
October, November and December

And now, write the months here. There is a poem for remembering the months and the days of each month.
Helen—What is it, mother?
Mother—

Thirty days hath September,
April, June and November,
One has twenty-eight and the others, thirty-one.

WORD STUDY

boca (la)   **ojo (el)**   **brazo (el)**

LECCIÓN 37

LA FINCA DE LOS ABUELOS

Do you know that Spanish roosters don't say "cock a doodle doo"? You can't possibly guess what they do say—so you'll just have to listen.

Elena—Mamá, papá, ya veo la casa de los abuelos. Miren, allá está.
Papá—Tienes razón, Elena. Allá está. El abuelo está delante de la puerta.
Abuelo—Dejen el auto aquí. Pasen, pasen.
Abuela—Queridos, bienvenidos. ¿Ésta es Elena? No lo creo. ¡Cómo crece esta niña! Y Carlitos—¿ya camina sólo?
Mamá—Sí, mamá. Camina sólo y corre por la casa.
Abuelo—Vamos a dar un paseo por la finca mientras hay luz.
Papá—Magnífica idea. ¿Vienes con nosotros, Clara?
Mamá—No, ve con Elena y Carlitos. Enséñales todos los animales a los niños.
Elena—Abuelo, ¿cómo se llama este animal?
Abuelo—Se llama burro.
Elena—Abuelo, ¿cómo se llama éste?
Abuelo—Se llama toro.
Elena—¿Qué dice el cerdo, abuelo?
Abuelo—¡Ja, ja! Dice, "Oinc, oinc."
Carlitos—Oinc, oinc.
Elena—¿Qué dicen los gallos?
Abuelo—Dicen "quiquiriquí."
Elena—¿Cuántas gallinas tienes, abuelo?
Abuelo—Hay cuarenta y ocho gallinas.
Papá—Y ¡cuántas casitas nuevas en la finca!
Abuelo—Hacemos lo que podemos. ¿Quieres oír una canción de mi finca?

Vengan a ver mi finca
Que es hermosa
Vengan a ver mi finca
Que es hermosa
Los pollitos hacen así
Pío, pío
Los pollitos hacen así
Pío, pío
¡Oh, ven camarad oh, ven camarad,
Oh ven, oh ven, oh ven
¡Oh, ven camarad oh, ven camarad,
Oh ven, oh ven, oh ven!

LESSON 37

GRANDPARENTS' FARM

Helen—Mother, Father, I see Grandfather's house already. Look, there it is.

Father—You're right Helen. There it is. Grandfather is in front of the door.

Grandfather—Leave the auto here. Enter, enter.

Grandmother—Darlings, welcome. This is Helen? I don't believe it. How this girl grows! And Charlie, does he walk alone yet?

Mother—Yes, Mother. He walks alone and runs through the house.

Grandfather—Let's take a walk through the farm while it's light.

Father—Magnificent idea. Are you coming with us, Clara?

Mother—No. Go with Helen and Charlie. Show the children all the animals.

Helen—Grandfather. What's the name of this animal?

Grandfather—It's called a donkey.

Helen—Grandfather, what is the name of this one?

Grandfather—It is called a bull.

Helen—What does the pig say, Grandfather?

Grandfather—Ha, ha. He says, "oink, oink."

Charlie—Oink, oink.

Helen—What do the roosters say?

Grandfather—They say "cock-a-doodle-doo."

Helen—How many chickens do you have, Grandfather!

Grandfather—There are forty-eight chickens.

Father—And how many new little houses on the farm!

Grandfather—We do what we can. Do you want to hear a song of my farm?

Come to see my "little farm"
Because it is beautiful
Come to see my "little farm"
Because it is beautiful
The little chicks do thus
Peep Peep
The little chicks do thus
Peep Peep
Oh come comrade, oh come comrade
Oh come, oh come, oh come
Oh come, comrade, oh come comrade
Oh come, oh come, oh come.

WORD STUDY

circo (el) **león (el)** **payaso (el)**

90

LECCIÓN 38

¡QUIQUIRIQUÍ!

What thoughts come into your head when you see a big orange pumpkin? Pumpkin pie or—? What do you think Helen wants to do with the pumpkin she finds on her grandparents' farm?

Elena—Mamá, ¿puedo dar un paseo por la finca más tarde?

Mamá—Sí, Elena, después del desayuno. La abuelita prepara siempre cosas buenas para el desayuno.

Elena—Vamos a bajar a la cocina. Tengo mucha hambre.

Elena—Muchas gracias, abuela. Todo está delicioso.

Abuela—De nada, Elena.

Elena—Abuela, ¿tienes una canasta? Quiero coger hojas para llevar a mi escuela.

Abuela—¡Cómo no! Aquí tienes una canasta grande.

Papá—Yo voy contigo, Elena.

Abuelo—Y yo también.

Elena—Papá, papá, mira las calabazas. Son enormes. Abuelo, ¿puedo coger una y cortarle los ojos y la nariz y la boca?

Abuelo—Sí, cómo no.

Elena—¿Y puedo meterle una vela y ponerla en mi ventana como hacen en los Estados Unidos?

Abuelo—Sí, cómo no.

Papá—¿Tienes bastantes hojas para tu escuela?

Elena—Sí, papá, gracias.

Papá—Entonces, vamos a regresar. Vamos a jugar con Carlitos un rato.

Vamos a cantar:

Allá En El Rancho Grande

Allá en el rancho grande
Allá donde vivía
Había una rancherita
Que alegre me decía
Que alegre me decía
Te voy a hacer tus calzones
Como los usa el ranchero
Te los comienzo de lana
Te los acabo de cuero.

LESSON 38

COCK-A-DOODLE-DOO

Helen—Mother, may I take a walk through the farm later?
Mother—Yes, Helen. After breakfast. Grandmama always prepares good things for breakfast.
Helen—Let's go down to the kitchen. I'm very hungry.

Helen—Many thanks, Grandmother. Everything is delicious.
Grandmother—You're welcome, Helen.
Helen—Grandmother, do you have a basket? I want to pick leaves to take them to my school.
Grandmother—Of course. Here is a large basket.
Father—I'll go with you, Helen.
Grandfather—And I, too.
Helen—Father, Father. Look at the pumpkins. They're enormous. Grandfather, may I take one and cut the eyes, nose and mouth?

Grandfather—Yes, of course.
Helen—May I put a candle inside and place it in front of my window as they do in the United States?
Grandfather—Yes, gladly.

Father—Do you have enough leaves for your school?
Helen—Yes, Papa, thanks.
Father—Then, let's go back. Let's play with Charlie a while.

Let's Sing!

There at the big ranch
Where I lived
There was a little ranch girl
Who happily used to say to me,
I'm going to make you breeches
Like the ones the ranchers use.
I'll start them of wool
I'll finish them for you in leather.

WORD STUDY

primavera (la)

horno (el)

zapatillas (las)

cartero (el)

LECCIÓN 39

QUIERO UN ÁRBOL GRANDE, GRANDE

Christmas preparations are always fun, even when you can't have a tree that goes way up to the ceiling.

Elena—Mamá, ¿qué día es hoy?
Mamá—Es el quince de diciembre.
Elena—Mamá, ¿cuándo vamos a comprar el árbol de Navidad?
Mamá—¿Prefieres el árbol de Navidad en vez del Nacimiento?*
Elena—Sí, mamá. Quiero un árbol grande como el año pasado.
Mamá—Hazme el favor de buscar los globitos y los adornos del arbol.

Elena—¿Dónde están, mamá?
Mamá—Hay tres cajas grandes en la parte baja de mi armario.

Elena—Aquí está la primera caja. ¿Dónde la pongo?
Mamá—Aquí en la mesa.
Elena—Vamos a contar los globitos. Hay cuarenta y dos.
Mamá—Tenemos que comprar una docena más.
Elena—¿Puedo comprarlos, mamá? Yo quiero globitos rojos y azules y amarillos y verdes, o globitos de todos colores.
Mamá—Ve a traer la segunda caja.
Elena—¡Qué adornos tan lindos! Esta estrella es muy bonita.
Mamá—Ve a traer la otra caja, Elena.
Elena—¡Cuántas luces, mamá!
Elena—Entonces, mamá, ¿qué tengo que comprar?
Mamá—Una docena de globitos de varios colores.
Elena—¿De qué tamaño, mamá? ¿Grandes, medianos o pequeños?
Mamá—Medianos. Compra también tres luces más y un paquete de nieve artificial.
Elena—Bueno. Mamá, ¿vienen los abuelos a pasar las fiestas con nosotros?
Mamá—Sí, seguro que sí. Pero llama a tus abuelos por teléfono.
Elena—¿Cómo, mamá?
Mamá—Di a la señorita: "Quiero 2458 (dos cuatro cinco ocho) en Chihuahua."

Elena—Abuelita, abuelita. Vengan a pasar las fiestas de Navidad con nosotros. ¿Verdad? Gracias, abuelita, gracias.

* Referring to the customs of North and South America.

LESSON 39

I WANT A BIG, BIG TREE

Helen—Mother, what day is today?
Mother—It's the fifteenth of December.
Helen—Mother, when are we going to buy the Christmas tree?
Mother—Do you prefer the Christmas Tree to the Nativity Scene°?
Helen—Yes, Mother. I want a big tree like the one last year.
Mother—But now, please look for the balls and trimmings for the tree.
Helen—Where are they, Mother?
Mother—There are three big boxes in my closet on the floor.

Helen—Here's the first box. Where shall I put it?
Mother—Here on the table.
Helen—Let's count the balls. There are forty-two of them.
Mother—We have to buy a dozen more.
Helen—May I buy them, Mother? I want red, blue, yellow and green balls—balls of all colors.
Mother—Go and get the second box.
Helen—What beautiful trimmings! This star is very pretty.
Mother—Go and get the other box, Helen.
Helen—How many lights, Mother! So, Mother, what do we have to buy?
Mother—A dozen balls of various colors.
Helen—Of what size, Mother? Large, medium or small?
Mother—Medium. Also buy three more lights and a package of artificial snow.
Helen—All right, Mother. Are our grandparents coming to spend the holidays with us?
Mother—Yes, certainly. But call your grandparents by phone.
Helen—How, Mama?
Mother—Say to the young lady, I want 2458 (dos cuatro cinco ocho) in Chihuahua.
Helen—Grandmother, Grandmother. You're coming to spend the Christmas holidays with us, aren't you? Thank you, Grandmother, thank you.

° Referring to the customs of North and South America.

FINAL QUIZ

You must know the answers to these. Let's see if you've earned your diploma. Turn to page 96 to check your answers.

1. ¿Cuál es la estación favorita de la señora Sanchez?
2. ¿Dónde viven los abuelos?
3. ¿Cuál es el número de teléfono de los abuelos?
4. ¿Como es el poema con los meses?
5. ¿Qué dice el gallo?
6. ¿Cuántos cajas de adornos hay?
7. ¿Cuántos globitos hay?
8. ¿Qué tiene que comprar Elena?
9. ¿En qué grado está, Elena?
10. ¿Cómo cantamos "Jingle Bells" en español?

LECCIÓN 40

FELIZ NAVIDAD Y FELIZ AÑO NUEVO

Did you know that Santa Claus doesn't bring presents to children in all lands? But—don't feel sorry for the children. They receive presents anyway. Let's find out how.

Abuelo—El árbol está muy lindo con todas las luces.
Elena—Yo he comprado estos globitos. ¿Te gustan, abuelito?
Abuelo—Me gustan mucho.
Abuela—¡Cuántas tarjetas de Navidad!
Elena—Mira ésta, abuelita, con Papá Noel.
Abuela—¿Sabes leerla, Elena?
Elena—¡Ja, ja! Sí, abuelita, yo voy a la escuela. Estoy en el tercer grado.
Abuela—Entonces, vamos a ver. Léela.
Elena—"Feliz Navidad y Feliz Año Nuevo a nuestros queridos amigos Clara y Carlos y a sus hijos Elena y Carlitos."
Abuela—Muy bien. Mira ésta con los Reyes Magos en sus camellos.
Elena—¿Cómo se dice en inglés "Los Reyes Magos"?
Abuela—"The Three Wise Men." Sabes, Elena, tienes suerte. Como tu abuelita viene de los Estados Unidos, celebramos dos navidades. Recibes regalos de Papá Noel el veinte y cinco de diciembre y recibes regalos de los Reyes Magos el seis de enero.
Elena—¡Los regalos, los regalos! ¿No es ya hora de abrir los regalos?
Abuelo—Todavía no. No es aún la **medianoche**. Faltan diez minutos.
Papá—Es la medianoche. Feliz Navidad, todos.
Todos—Feliz Navidad.
Elena—¿Puedo abrir mis regalos, mamá, por favor?
Mamá—Sí, Elena. Abre éste primero.
Elena—Una muñeca que camina y que **habla**. ¡Oh, gracias, gracias! Un coche azul para la muñeca. ¡Oh, gracias, gracias!
¡Oh, qué lindos! Un par de patines . . . ¡Oh, gracias, gracias a todos y Feliz Navidad! ¿Podemos cantar ahora?
Todos—

Cascabeles, cascabeles
Tra, la, la, la, la
¡Qué alegría todo el día!
Tra, la, la, la, la.
Cascabeles, cascabeles
Tra, la, la, la, la
¡Qué alegría todo el día!
Tra, la, la, la, la.

LESSON 40

MERRY CHRISTMAS AND HAPPY NEW YEAR

Grandfather—The tree is very pretty with all the lights.
Helen—I bought these balls. Do you like them, Grandfather?
Grandfather—I like them very much.
Grandmother—How many Christmas cards!
Helen—Look at this one, Grandmother, with Santa Claus.
Grandmother—Do you know how to read it, Helen?
Helen—Ha, ha. Yes, Grandmother. I go to school. I'm in the third grade.
Grandmother—So. Let's see. Read it.
Helen—Merry Christmas and Happy New Year to our dear friends Clara and Charles and their children Helen and Charlie.
Grandmother—Very good. Look at this one with the "Wise Men" on their camels.
Helen—How do you say "the Wise Men" in English?
Grandmother—The Three Wise Men. You know Helen you're lucky. Since your grandmother comes from the United States we celebrate two Christmases. You receive presents from Santa Claus on December 25th and presents from The Three Wise Men on the 6th of January.
Helen—Gifts, the gifts. Isn't it time to open the gifts?
Grandfather—Not yet. It's not midnight. There are ten minutes yet.
Father—It's midnight. Merry Christmas everyone.
All—Merry Christmas.
Helen—May I open my gifts, Mother, please?
Mother—Yes, Helen. Open this one first.
Helen—A doll which walks and talks. Oh thanks, thanks.
 A blue carriage for the doll. Oh thanks, thanks.
 Oh, how pretty! A pair of skates. Oh thanks, thanks, everyone, and Merry Christmas. Can we sing now?

Everyone { Jingle Bells, Jingle Bells
Tra, la, la, la, la
What joy all day
Tra, la, la, la, la.

ANSWERS TO FINAL QUIZ

1. Es la primavera.
2. Viven en el campo.
3. Es Chihuahua dos—cuatro—cinco—ocho.
4. Treinta días trae septiembre con abril, junio y noviembre. Veinte y ocho tiene uno y los demás treinta y uno.
5. Dice qui qui ri quí.
6. Hay tres cajas.
7. Hay cuarenta y dos globitos.
8. Tiene que comprar globitos, luces y un paquete de nieve artificial.
9. Está en el tercer grado.
10. Cantamos:
    Cascabeles, cascabeles,
    Tra, la, la, la, la,
    Qué alegría todo el día,
    Tra, la, la, la, la.